GCSE

Oxford Literature Companions

A Christmas Carol

CHARLES DICKENS

WORKBOOK

Notes and activities: Carmel Waldron
Series consultant: Peter Buckroyd

OXFORD

UNIVERSITY PRESS

Contents

What are Oxford Literature Companions?

Oxford Literature Companions is a series designed to provide you with comprehensive support for popular set texts. You can use the Companion workbook alongside your novel, using relevant sections during your studies or using the workbook as a whole for revision. The workbook will help you to create your own personalized guide to the text.

What are the main features within this workbook?

Each workbook in the Oxford Literature Companion series follows the same approach and includes the following features:

Activities

Each workbook offers a range of varied and in-depth activities to deepen understanding and encourage close work with the text, covering characters, themes, language and context. The Skills and Practice chapter also offers advice on assessment and includes sample questions and student answers. There are spaces to write your answers throughout the workbook.

Key quotation

Key terms and quotations

Throughout the workbook, key terms are highlighted in the text and explained on the same page. There is also a detailed glossary at the end of the workbook that explains, in the context of the novel, all the relevant literary terms highlighted.

Quotations from the novel appear in blue text throughout this workbook.

Upgrade

As well as providing guidance on key areas of the novel, throughout this workbook you will also find 'Upgrade' features. These are tips to help with your exam preparation and performance.

Progress check

Each chapter of the workbook ends with a 'Progress check'. Through self-assessment, these enable you to establish how confident you feel about what you have been learning and help you to set next steps and targets.

Which edition of the novel has this workbook used?

Quotations have been taken from the Oxford University Press Rollercoaster edition of *A Christmas Carol* (978-019-832998-5).

Plot and Structure

Plot

The title *A Christmas Carol* suggests a festive song and the novel is divided like a song with five verses or a piece of music with five staves.

Stave 1

The reader is introduced to Ebenezer Scrooge and his dead partner, Jacob Marley, on Christmas Eve.

Activity 1

a) At the start of the story, Scrooge is presented in connection with Marley. We are told several things about him in this relationship. Find a quotation that supports each one.

 i. That he signed the death certificate.

 ----

 ii. That he was the only person involved in Marley's affairs.

 ----

 iii. That on the day of the funeral he was carrying out business.

 ----

 iv. That he left Marley's name painted on the office door.

 ----

 v. That he acted as both partners after Marley's death.

 ----

b) What do you think Dickens wanted to show about Scrooge's relationship with Marley?

As the stave continues, the reader learns more about the way Scrooge treats others.

Activity 2

Look at how Scrooge treats people in Stave 1. For each of the following find a quotation and say what it shows about the way Dickens presents Scrooge and how this sets the scene for Scrooge's 'learning'.

Name	Quotation	What it shows about Scrooge
Bob Cratchit, his clerk		
Fred, his nephew		
The two charity collectors		
The carol singer		

After dining alone and spending an evening reading his banker's book, Scrooge goes home.

Activity 3

a) List in order the four spooky things that happen to Scrooge from his arrival at his house.

i. --

ii. --

iii. --

iv. --

b) Look at the quotations below describing Scrooge's reactions to the ghost in Stave 1. Use numbers 1–5 to put them in order showing how his reactions change. In each case explain what causes the change.

Quotation	Order (1-5)	Explanation
'Scrooge fell upon his knees, and clasped his hands before his face.'		
'Scrooge trembled more and more.'		
"You don't believe in me," observed the Ghost.		
'He tried to say "Humbug!" but stopped at the first syllable.'		
'Scrooge's countenance fell almost as low as the Ghost's had done.'		

Marley's ghost has come to warn Scrooge of what awaits him in the afterlife unless he changes his ways.

Activity 4

a) Dickens presents the spirit of Marley as a conventional ghost. Comment on where and how Dickens uses each traditional feature.

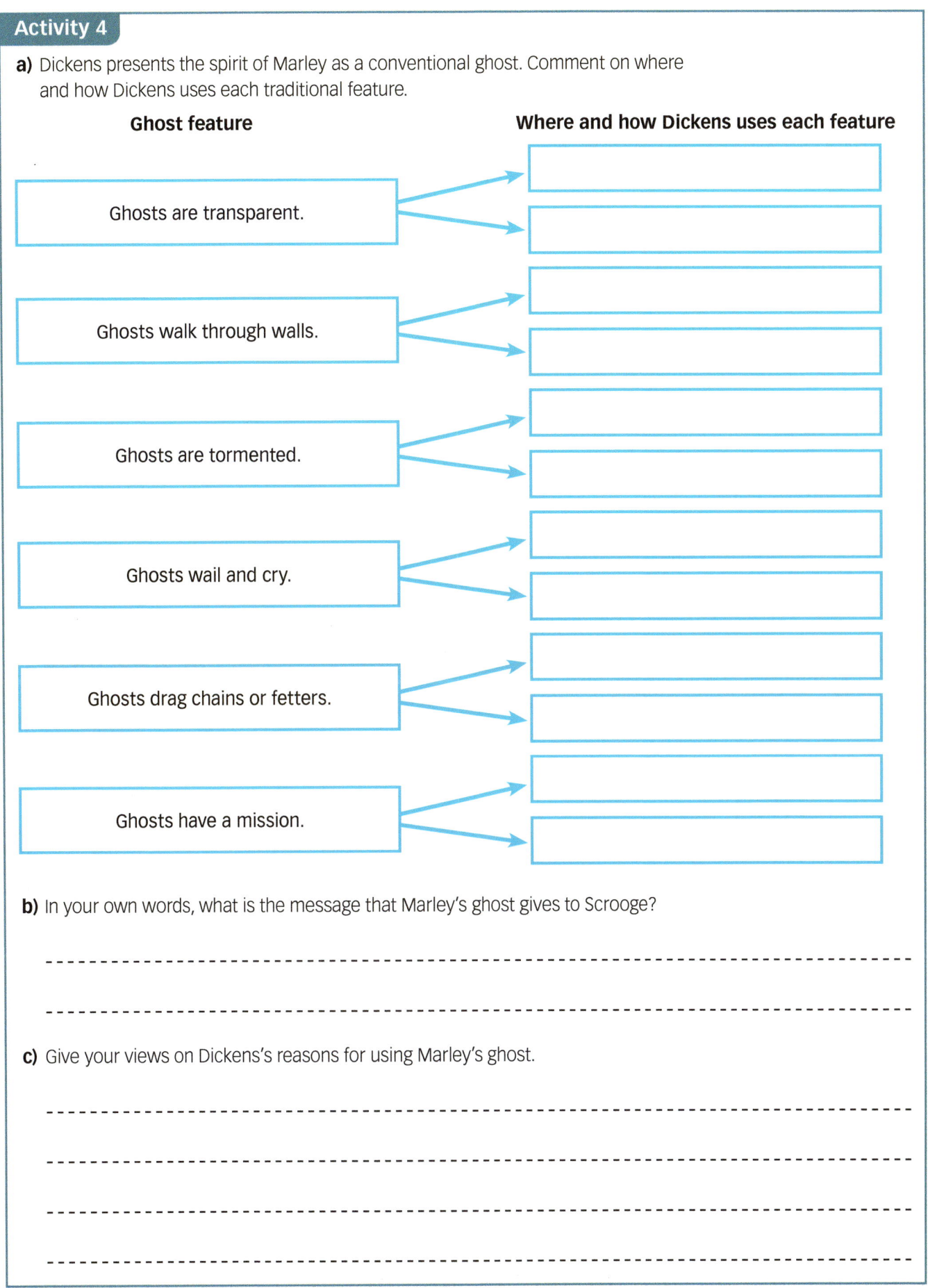

Ghost feature

Where and how Dickens uses each feature

Ghosts are transparent.

Ghosts walk through walls.

Ghosts are tormented.

Ghosts wail and cry.

Ghosts drag chains or fetters.

Ghosts have a mission.

b) In your own words, what is the message that Marley's ghost gives to Scrooge?

----

c) Give your views on Dickens's reasons for using Marley's ghost.

The novella is written in the third person – that is, from the point of view of a narrator who is not a character, but who can see the actions, thoughts and feelings of all the characters.

Activity 5

As an all-seeing narrator, Dickens can use different viewpoints within the text to advance the plot, and can even have the narrator give his own opinions. Look at the following quotations and group them under the three headings in the table below.

"Marley was dead, to begin with." *(Stave 1)*

"I don't mean to say that I know, of my own knowledge, what there is particularly dead about a door-nail." *(Stave 1)*

"But what did Scrooge care! It was the very thing he liked." *(Stave 1)*

"Seeing clearly that it would be useless to pursue their point, the gentlemen withdrew." *(Stave 1)*

"…the clerk…went down a slide on Cornhill, at the end of a lane of boys, twenty times…" *(Stave 1)*

"And then let any man explain to me, if he can…" *(Stave 1)*

"As Scrooge looked fixedly at this phenomenon, it was a knocker again." *(Stave 1)*

Narrator telling the story	Viewpoint of a character (say which)	Narrator's own opinion

Stave 2

The first of the promised spirits arrives – the Ghost of Christmas Past.
This spirit represents memory and takes Scrooge on a journey into his past.

Activity 6

a) Make a list of the scenes that the spirit visits with Scrooge.

----

b) Why do you think Dickens begins Scrooge's reformation with memories of his past?

By finding clues in the text, the reader can see how Dickens slowly breaks
down Scrooge's selfish and uncaring attitudes, preparing the way for his final
redemption. In this stave it is through his memories of his past life.

Activity 7

Look at Scrooge's visit to his old school and complete the spider diagram showing the thoughts and feelings it arouses in him. Add a brief quotation as evidence for each one.

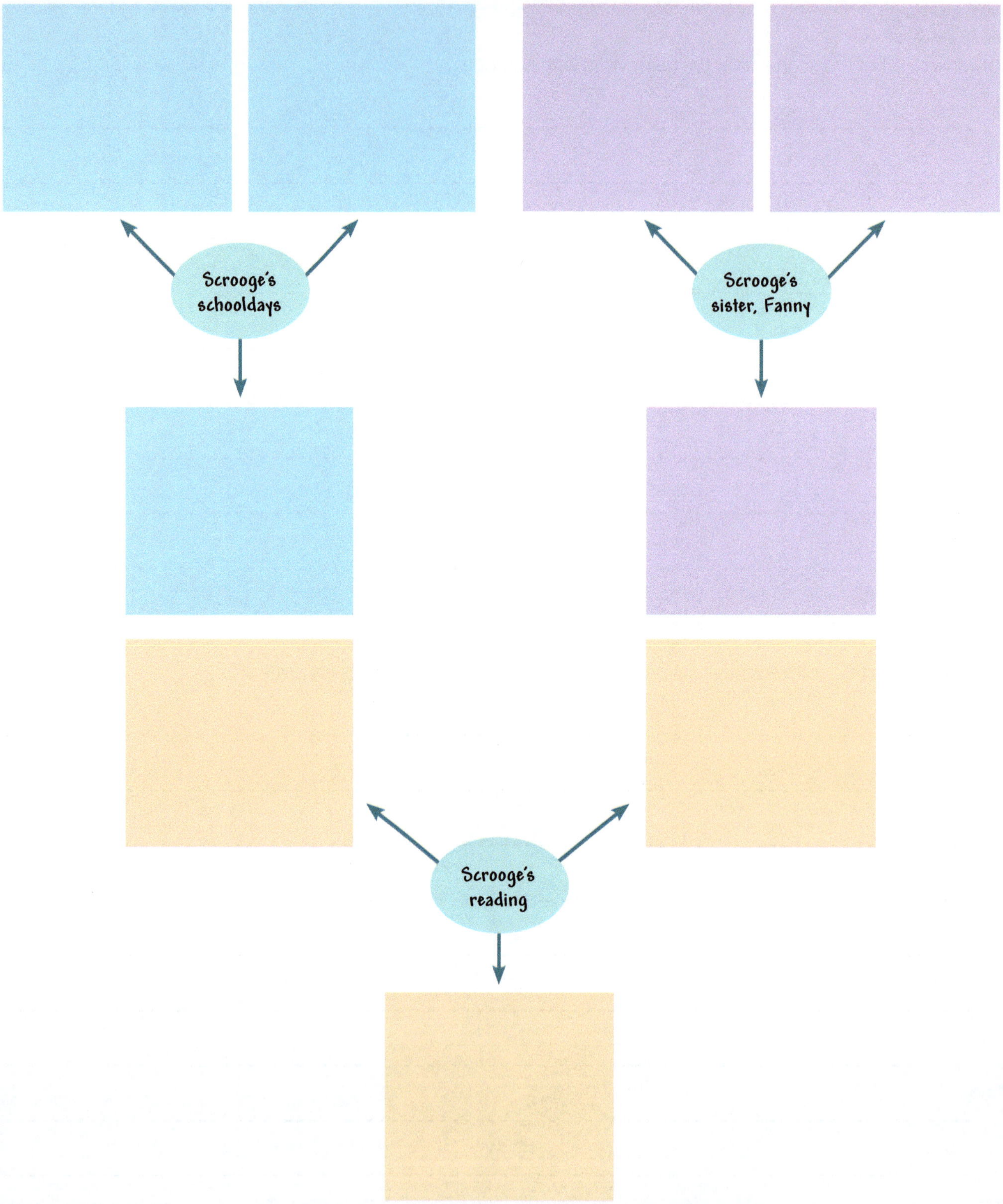

Scrooge's
schooldays

Scrooge's
sister, Fanny

Scrooge's
reading

It is useful to make brief notes on the way that Dickens introduces clues to Scrooge's human side so that you can trace his moral and spiritual journey through the book.

The next place the ghost takes him is to his first place of employment as an apprentice. They arrive as his employer, Fezziwig, is giving a big Christmas Eve party for his neighbours and employees.

Activity 8

Look at the following quotations from Scrooge as he views the scene and suggest what they tell the reader about his state of mind.

a) "Why, it's old Fezziwig! Bless his heart; it's Fezziwig alive again!" *(Stave 2)*

- -

b) "He was very much attached to me, was Dick. Poor Dick! Dear, dear!" *(Stave 2)*

- -

c) "The happiness he gives, is quite as great as if it cost a fortune." *(Stave 2)*

- -

d) "I should like to be able to say a word or two to my clerk just now. That's all." *(Stave 2)*

- -

The spirit's final trip to Scrooge's past shows his fiancée, Belle, breaking off their engagement.

Activity 9

a) Which of the reasons below does Belle give for breaking off the engagement?
Tick those you agree with and give reasons for your choices.

She doesn't love him any more		She wants to marry someone rich	

-   -

They no longer have anything in common		It was her father's idea but now he is dead she can choose	

-   -

He is too obsessed with making money		She thinks he will be better off without her	

-   -

b) The spirit forces Scrooge to observe Belle's happiness with the man she married and their children. Write three reasons on separate paper why the ghost shows Scrooge this scene, although it is not part of his memory.

11

Stave 3

Scrooge meets the Ghost of Christmas Present, who takes him on a journey through the streets, where shoppers mingle with the poor people taking their dinners to be cooked in the bakers' ovens. They visit the Cratchit family for Christmas dinner and then travel to lonely places to observe the Christmas spirit abroad. They finish their journey at Fred's Christmas party, to which Scrooge refused to go.

Activity 10

a) Look at the description of the spirit's throne in paragraph 5 of Stave 3. Then look at the descriptions of the fruiterers and the grocers further on. For each description write a list of items mentioned under the appropriate headings.

Throne	Fruiterers	Grocers

b) Write a paragraph about the way Dickens uses lists to create the effect of a generous abundance.

A conversation about the poor people who are taking their dinners to the bakers to use their ovens as they have none of their own leads to the next scene, in the Cratchit house.

Activity 11

Read the section of the text in Stave 3 where Bob Cratchit's family celebrate Christmas. They are a caring family and all help to look after Tiny Tim.

Now look at the following quotations and comment on the ways Dickens presents Scrooge changing in this episode.

"Spirit," said Scrooge, with an interest he had never felt before, "tell me if Tiny Tim will live."

"No, no," said Scrooge. "Oh, no, kind Spirit! say he will be spared."

Tiny Tim

'Scrooge hung his head to hear his own words quoted by the Spirit, and was overcome with penitence and grief.'

'Scrooge bent before the Ghost's rebuke, and trembling cast his eyes upon the ground.'

'Scrooge had his eye upon them, and especially on Tiny Tim, until the last.'

The spirit whisks Scrooge across streets full of people visiting each other and out across bleak moorland, a rocky headland with a lighthouse and a churning sea to a lonely ship.

Activity 12

Dickens contrasts the inhospitable terrain with the comradeship in people's hearts as they celebrate the season.

For each quotation about the terrain below, fill in a contrasting quotation about the people in the matching speech bubble.

'...nothing grew but moss and furze, and coarse rank grass.'

'Built upon a dismal reef of sunken rocks, some league or so from shore...'

'Again the Ghost sped on, above the black and heaving sea—on, on...'

Scrooge hears his nephew laughing and finds himself at Fred's Christmas party. Everyone is enjoying themselves, eating and drinking and playing games.

Activity 13

a) Think about the way Dickens presents Scrooge in this episode and answer the questions below, including a brief quotation as evidence.

   i. How does the tune that his niece plays on the harp affect Scrooge?

---

   ii. What is Scrooge's reaction to the game of 'How, When and Where' that his niece is good at?

---

iii. What favour does Scrooge ask the Spirit of Christmas Present that it says cannot be done?

----

iv. What is Scrooge tempted to do when his nephew toasts him?

----

b) Look at your answers to the questions above and write a comment on the changes in Scrooge's attitude.

----

c) Why do you think Dickens chooses to end this stave not on the good cheer of Fred's party but with the discovery of the two children, Want and Ignorance?

Stave 4

The Ghost of Christmas Yet to Come leads Scrooge without speaking. Scrooge is now willing to learn and tries to make sense of what the ghost shows him.

Activity 14

The spirit directs Scrooge to conversations between his colleagues following the death of someone the reader guesses to be Scrooge.

a) The four men he overhears at the Royal Exchange have just heard the news. What do the following phrases suggest about their feelings?

Overheard phrases	What they suggest
"I don't know much about it, either way. I only know he's dead."	
"God knows," said the first, with a yawn.	
'This pleasantry was received with a general laugh.'	
"It's likely to be a very cheap funeral"	
"I don't mind going if a lunch is provided"	
"But I'll offer to go, if anybody else will."	

b) Now read the exchange between the two men in the street who are wealthy businessmen Scrooge tried to impress, below:

"Well!" said the first. "Old Scratch has got his own at last, hey?"
"So I am told," returned the second. "Cold, isn't it?"

This is all their interest in his death. What is Dickens saying here about Scrooge's attitude to money?

The spirit takes Scrooge into the worst part of town where crime and squalor are rife, and shows three people selling items they have stolen from a dead man to a dealer in stolen goods.

Activity 15

a) Compare the two death scenes in Stave 4. How does Dickens show the contrast between Scrooge's death and that of Tiny Tim? Think about:

   i. The atmosphere of the room where the body lies

   ii. The conversation about the dead person

   iii. The description of feelings caused by the death

   iv. The place where they are being buried

b) Why do you think Dickens presents Scrooge as being unaware that the dead man is himself?

Stave 5

Scrooge's relief at finding himself alive and it being Christmas morning is profound.
He is determined to become a different person and to help others and enjoy his life.

 Activity 16

Dickens uses several ways of expressing Scrooge's feelings. Find three words or
phrases he writes to show these feelings through the following:

a) The way Scrooge gets dressed

----

b) The way he speaks out loud

----

c) The way he laughs

----

d) The sound of the church bells

----

e) The weather

In the exam you should look in detail at the way the writer uses word and language techniques to create effects. You should learn a small selection of these by heart, so that you can use them if the question is appropriate.

For example, look at the sentence: 'He went to church, and walked about the streets, and watched the people hurrying to and fro, and patted children on the head, and questioned beggars, and looked down into the kitchens of houses, and up to the windows, and found that everything could yield him pleasure.'

The structure of several clauses all joined by 'and' gives an impression of hurrying to make up for lost time, while the use of action verbs, 'went', 'walked', 'watched', 'patted', 'questioned', 'looked' and 'found', all suggest a new involvement with other people.

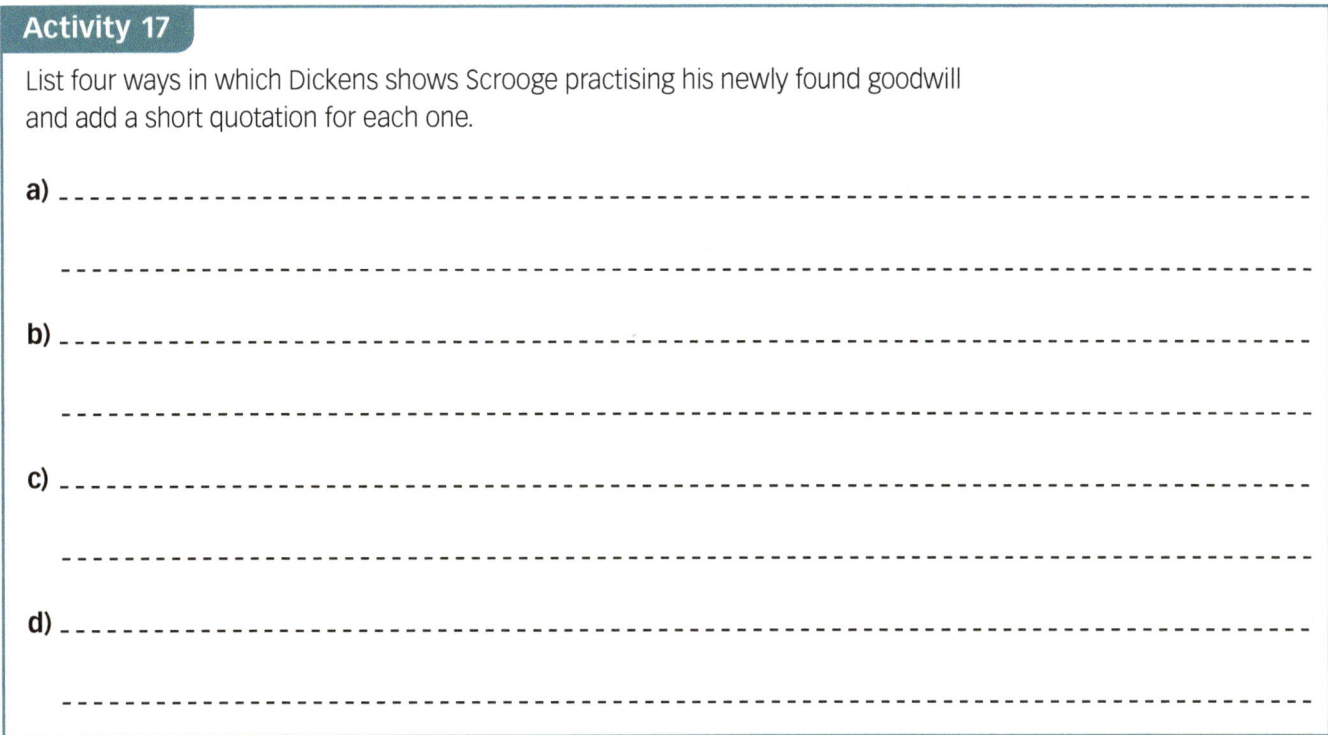

Activity 17

List four ways in which Dickens shows Scrooge practising his newly found goodwill and add a short quotation for each one.

a) --

  ----

b) --

  ----

c) --

  ----

d) --

Structure

A Christmas Carol is a novella that follows the idea of a poem or carol with five verses. That is why it is divided into staves rather than chapters. It is a story about an old miser who finds redemption with the aid of ghosts. It is also a tale about the need for social justice and reform. At its heart it is a carol about the power of kindness and family love. Charles Dickens's ghost story is largely responsible for the way in which Christmas is viewed today.

The outline of the plot also follows a typical five-act structure of **exposition, rising action, climax, falling action or resolution**, and **denouement**, known as Freytag's pyramid.

climax the high point or peak of the action, after which everything changes

denouement the way the main character finally ends up (happily in comedy; badly in tragedy)

exposition where the author introduces the main character and the basic conflict, finishing with the event that decides the rest of the story

falling action or resolution the final part of the conflict that decides whether the main character wins or loses

rising action the series of events that lead in stages up to the story's climax

Activity 18

Freytag's pyramid is a diagram that shows the structure of a story, be it a novel, play or film.

Write in and around the boxes on each part of the pyramid, to show how *A Christmas Carol* fits this structure.

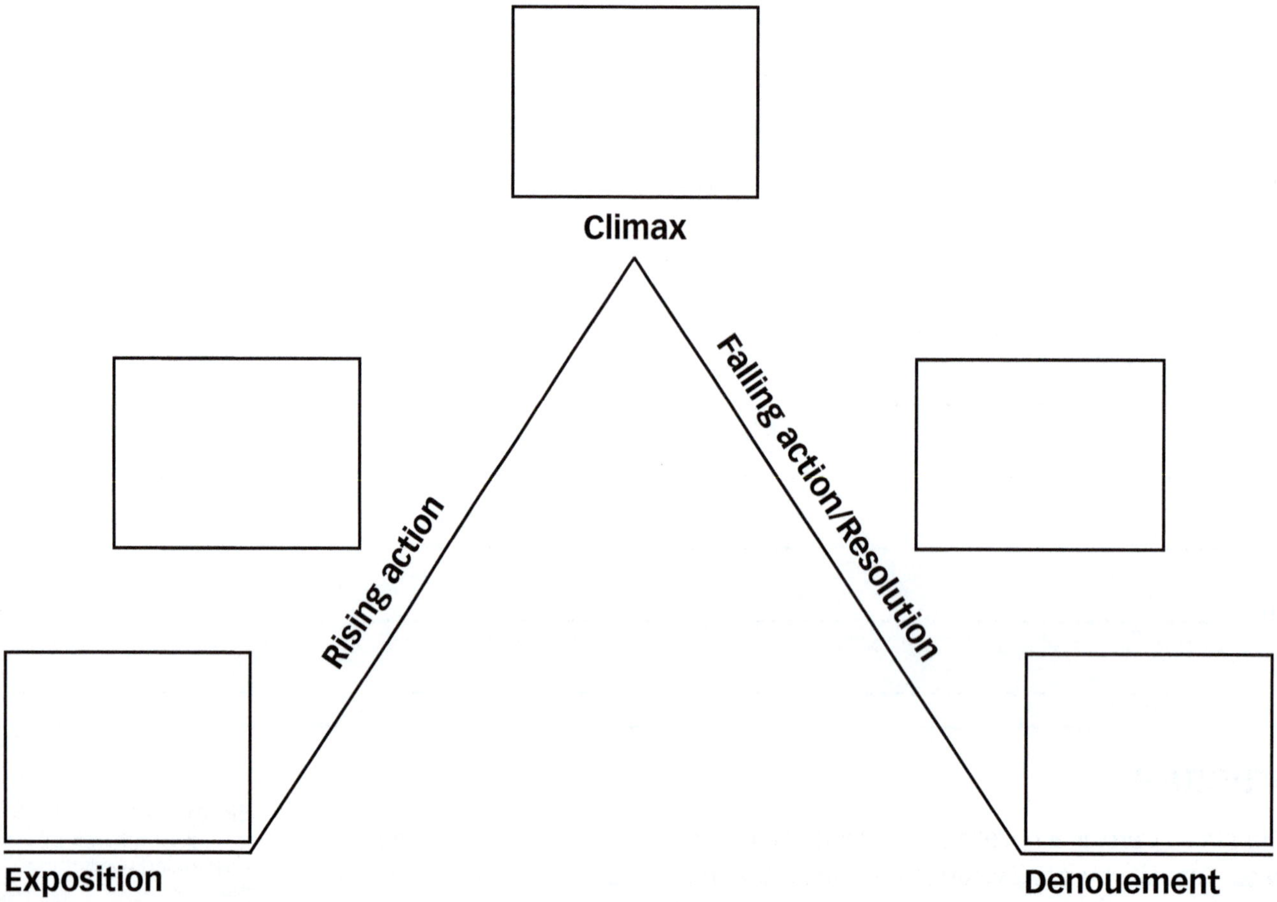

Climax

Falling action/Resolution

Rising action

Exposition

Denouement

Dickens uses a double timescale in the novella as the action all takes place on Christmas Eve, but it also covers Scrooge's lifetime – past, present and future.

Activity 19

Complete the boxes below to show the structure of the play. Include the events in chronological order to create a double timeline.

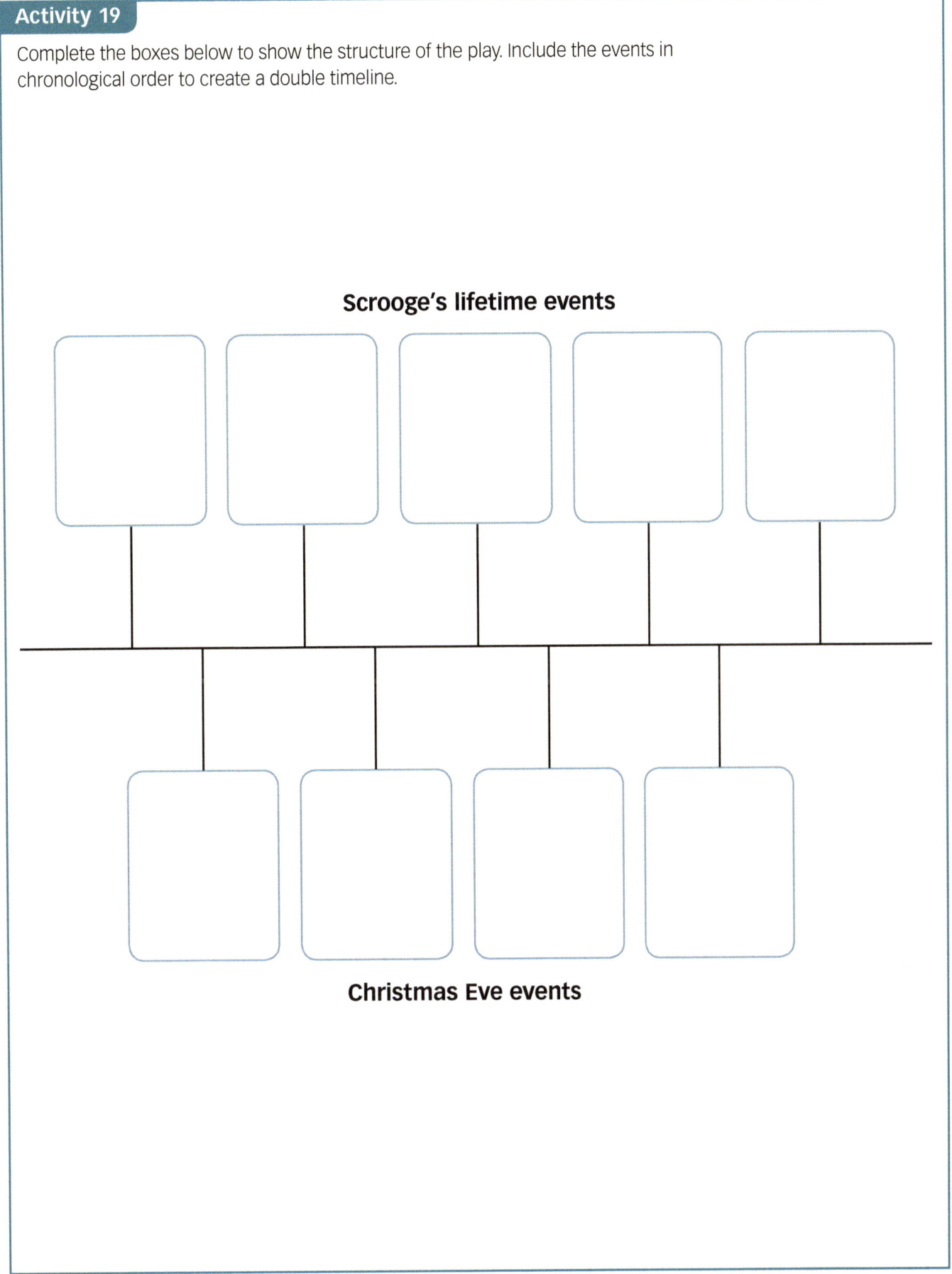

Scrooge's lifetime events

Christmas Eve events

The setting of *A Christmas Carol* is London, although Scrooge's mysterious journeys with the ghosts widen the impression to create a more universal setting.

 Activity 20

Look at the following quotations and write a paragraph about how Dickens presents the city.

> 'The fog came pouring in at every chink and keyhole, and was so dense without, that although the court was of the narrowest, the houses opposite were mere phantoms.' *(Stave 1)*

> 'The water-plug being left in solitude, its overflowings sullenly congealed, and turned to misanthropic ice.' *(Stave 1)*

> '...the smooth white sheet of snow upon the roofs, and with the dirtier snow upon the ground...' *(Stave 3)*

> '...the shortest streets were choked up with a dingy mist, half thawed, half frozen, whose heavier particles descended in a shower of sooty atoms...' *(Stave 3)*

Progress check

Use the chart below to review the skills you have developed in this chapter. For each column, start at the bottom box and work your way up towards the highest level in the top box. Tick the box to show you have achieved that level.

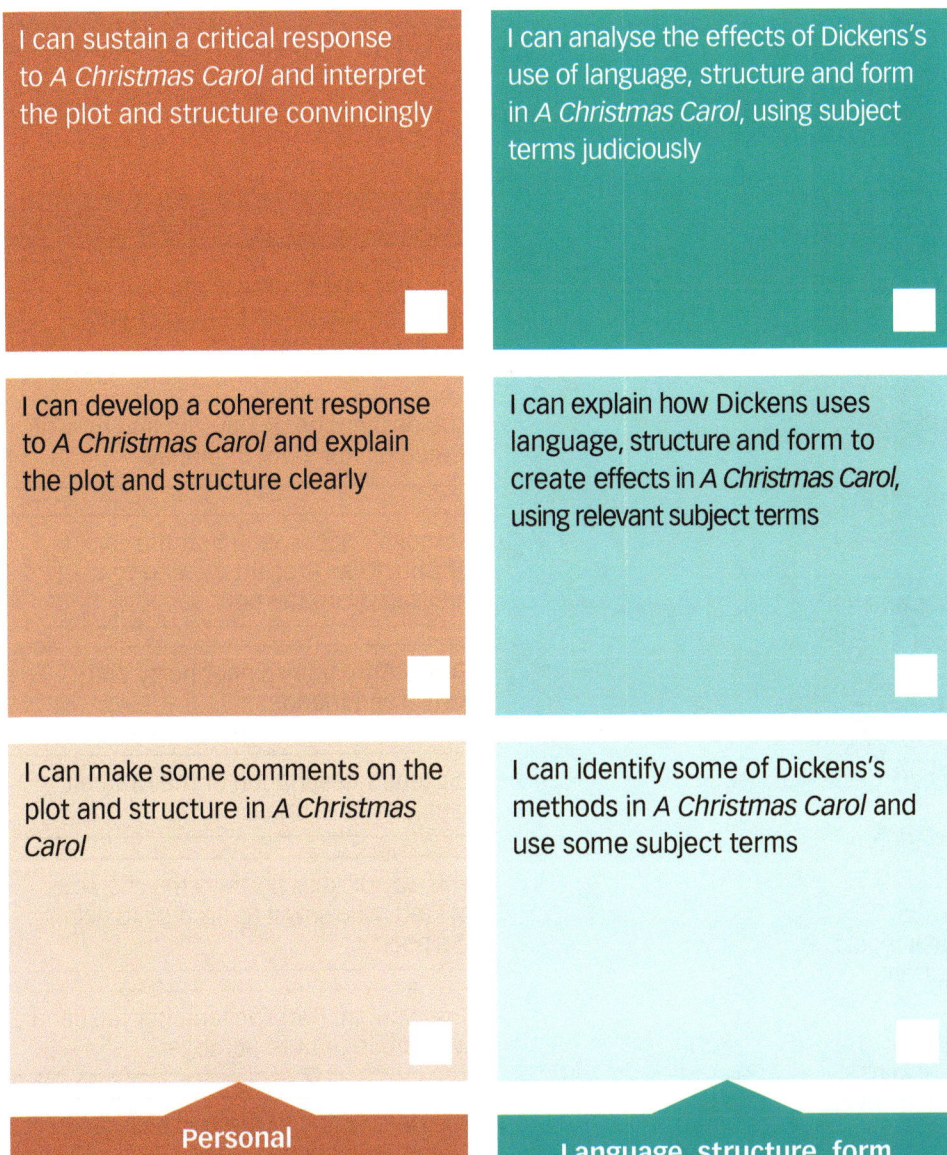

I can sustain a critical response to *A Christmas Carol* and interpret the plot and structure convincingly

I can analyse the effects of Dickens's use of language, structure and form in *A Christmas Carol*, using subject terms judiciously

I can develop a coherent response to *A Christmas Carol* and explain the plot and structure clearly

I can explain how Dickens uses language, structure and form to create effects in *A Christmas Carol*, using relevant subject terms

I can make some comments on the plot and structure in *A Christmas Carol*

I can identify some of Dickens's methods in *A Christmas Carol* and use some subject terms

Personal response

Language, structure, form

Charles Dickens

Charles Dickens had a difficult childhood and was always sympathetic to children and others who suffered through no fault of their own. As with many other authors, some of his own experiences are reflected in his novels, including *A Christmas Carol*.

Activity 1

Decide how incidents in Dickens's life compare with incidents or ideas in *A Christmas Carol*. Draw connecting lines between the two.

Dickens's life	A Christmas Carol
The Dickens family was large but not well off. His father was a clerk.	The way that Scrooge (and Marley when he was alive) treated charity collectors and the poor.
When Dickens had his own family he made sure Christmases were special.	The description of Tiny Tim and how he would die for want of money.
Dickens was taken out of school at the age of 12.	Scrooge's accusation that the Ghost of Christmas Present wanted to take pleasure from the poor.
Dickens's family were very poor and he had to work in a factory, which he hated.	Fred's Christmas dinner party with family and friends.
Later Dickens worked as an office boy and began to write. He often wrote about children who were poor and abandoned.	Dickens's description of the Cratchit family at Christmas.
Dickens visited the slums of London, often walking miles at night.	The way Dickens portrays the character of Fred, who saw it as his duty to help the poor.
Dickens also visited the ragged schools, which affected his view of poor and ignorant youth.	The woman, Caroline, and her husband, who are in debt to Scrooge.
Although he was a Christian, Dickens saw nothing wrong with people enjoying themselves on Sunday.	The description of the two children 'Want' and 'Ignorance'.
Dickens supported a number of good causes, including Great Ormond Street Hospital for sick children.	The description Dickens gives of the dealer Old Joe, and his hovel in the slums.
As a writer Dickens criticized the division of society that made some people rich and others beggars.	Martha and Peter Cratchit worked to help the family finances.

Upgrade

You should show your knowledge of Charles Dickens's life through references to his own experiences only when you are using relevant material to answer an exam question. For example, his championing of the poor would be appropriate to include in a question on how poverty is presented in *A Christmas Carol*. Any points you make about context must always be linked to the text.

Victorian class and inequality

Victorian England had a rigid class structure, with the aristocracy at the top, followed by the middle class which included a wide range of occupations including clergymen, lawyers, army officers, manufacturers, bankers and other wealthy businessmen. Beneath them were the working class, which included clerks and teachers at this time. At the very bottom were the destitute and criminals.

Activity 2

a) Complete the table below by putting the following characters into the correct class:

Scrooge and Marley   Scrooge's colleagues   Fred   Bob Cratchit

Belle   Fezziwig   Old Joe   Want and Ignorance

For each one give a brief reason why you have included them in that class.

Class	Characters	Reasons
Wealthy middle class		
Less wealthy middle class		
Working class		
Destitute and criminal class		

Wealth and poverty

Dickens saw the division between those like Scrooge, who were wealthy but refused to use their money to help others, and Fred, who were far less wealthy but used their money and influence for good causes. Dickens himself used his money and influence as a popular writer to help others. *A Christmas Carol* itself seems to have had this effect. One fellow novelist, Margaret Oliphant, remarked "that in the days of its first publication it was regarded as 'a new gospel'" and noted that the book was unique in that it actually made people behave better.

Activity 3

Contrast how attitudes to poverty are shown in the story. Look at the following quotations and consider what each of them tells us about the speaker's attitude to poverty.

a)

"What right have you to be merry? What reason have you to be merry? You're poor enough." *(Scrooge, Stave 1)*

----

b)

"Many thousands are in want of common necessaries; hundreds of thousands are in want of common comforts, sir." *(Charity collector, Stave 1)*

----

c)

"The common welfare was my business; charity, mercy, forbearance, and benevolence, were, all, my business." *(Marley's Ghost, Stave 1)*

----

d)

"It was made when we were both poor and content to be so, until, in good season, we could improve our worldly fortune by our patient industry." *(Belle, Stave 2)*

----

e)

"But before that time we shall be ready with the money; and even though we were not, it would be a bad fortune indeed to find so merciless a creditor in his successor." *(Caroline's husband, Stave 4)*

----

f)

"Who's the worse for the loss of a few things like these? Not a dead man, I suppose." *(Charwoman, Stave 4)*

Victorian childhood

Living conditions

Children in Dickens's time were very vulnerable. If they survived birth and infancy, there were many diseases waiting for them. Middle-class children naturally had a stronger chance of surviving, while poor children who were living in slums with no proper sanitary arrangements and a dreadful diet were most likely to succumb.

Activity 4

At the same time as Dickens was writing *A Christmas Carol*, social researcher Henry Mayhew was documenting the life of London's poorer classes in *London Labour and the London Poor*:

> **Extract from *London Labour and the London Poor* by Henry Mayhew**
>
> The houses are of the poorest description, and seem as if they tumbled into their places at random. Foul channels, huge dust heaps, and a variety of other unsightly objects, occupy every open space, and dabbling among these are crowds of ragged dirty children who grub and wallow, as if in their native element.

Compare the above extract with Dickens's description in *A Christmas Carol*:

'The ways were foul and narrow; the shops and houses wretched; the people half-naked, drunken, slipshod, ugly. Alleys and archways, like so many cesspools, disgorged their offences of smell, and dirt, and life, upon the straggling streets; and the whole quarter reeked with crime, with filth, and misery.' *(Stave 4)*

What similarities can you find between these two descriptions in what they portray and the language they use to show it? Think about the following aspects and include a short quotation as evidence for your opinions.

a) The streets or alleys

----

b) The state of the houses

----

c) The condition of the people

----

d) The dirt surrounding them

Education

Dickens was convinced that the answer for children growing up in a poor environment was to educate them. However, Dickens was also aware that schools could be in poor conditions. Sometimes boys were abused in school, having been sent to board because their mothers had died and their fathers found it easier to send them to be educated and looked after at the same time.

Activity 5

Read this extract from a letter written by a young boy named Henry to his father in 1822, which he smuggled out without it being checked by his teacher. Compare it with the description of Scrooge's schooldays in Stave 2.

> **Extract from a young boy's letter to his father, 1822**
>
> …the letters you send me are all examined by Mr Smith before I see them, so I hope my dear Father you will mention nothing of this when you write – It is now two years come October since I left you at Islington, but I hope my dear Father you will let me come home at Xmas that we may once more meet again alive if God permit me to live as long. Our bread is nearly black it is made of the worst Barley Meal, and our Beds are stuffed with chaff and I assure you we are used more like Bears than Christians and believe me my dear Father I would rather be obliged to work all my life time than remain here another year.

a) Looking at these two experiences, list the similarities and differences between Henry's and Scrooge's experiences of school in the table below.

Similarities	Differences

b) What impression do you have of the boarding schools that less wealthy boys attended at this time?

----

c) What is your impression of the kind of education received by the Cratchit children?

Wealthy boys would be sent to be educated at Eton, Harrow, Rugby or Winchester. The less wealthy middle classes might go to the kind of schools attended by Henry and Scrooge. For poor children, there were far fewer educational opportunities and these were rather patchy as they depended on patrons and volunteers. There was no free educational provision by the government.

Victorian Christmas

By the time Dickens wrote *A Christmas Carol*, people were beginning to celebrate Christmas more as a holiday and a family occasion. The first Christmas card was sent in 1843, the year the novella was published.

Activity 6

What Christmas customs can you find in Dickens's presentation of Christmas in Stave 3? Complete the table below with at least one reference and one quotation.

Custom	How it is presented
Food and drink	
Holiday entertainments	
Giving and receiving	
Family gatherings	
Decorations	
Religious observance	

Activity 7

Read the speech that is given by Fred, explaining what Christmas means to him.

"But I am sure I have always thought of Christmas time, when it has come round—apart from the veneration due to its sacred name and origin, if anything belonging to it can be apart from that—as a good time; a kind, forgiving, charitable, pleasant time; the only time I know of, in the long calendar of the year, when men and women seem by one consent to open their shut-up hearts freely, and to think of people below them as if they really were fellow-passengers to the grave, and not another race of creatures bound on other journeys. And therefore, uncle, though it has never put a scrap of gold or silver in my pocket, I believe that it *has* done me good, and *will* do me good; and I say, God bless it!" *(Stave 1)*

For each of the following key phrases, complete this flow chart process:

explain what the phrase means	→	find an example from elsewhere in the story	→	give your opinion about the views expressed

a) "the veneration due to its sacred name and origin"

----

b) "a kind, forgiving, charitable, pleasant time"

----

c) "when men and women seem by one consent to open their shut-up hearts freely"

----

d) "think of people below them as if they really were fellow-passengers to the grave"

----

e) "another race of creatures bound on other journeys"

----

f) "it has never put a scrap of gold or silver in my pocket"

Activity 8

a) Look at the four pictures below of traditional Victorian Christmas customs.
For each of them find a suitable reference in *A Christmas Carol* and write a
quotation underneath.

Christmas giving

Christmas shopping

Christmas dinner

Christmas games

----

b) Using the information collected on page 31, and your knowledge of the text, summarise your thoughts about Christmas customs in *A Christmas Carol*. You should include:

- how Dickens presents the idea of a family gathering
- how he describes the shops and streets at Christmas
- his emphasis on generosity and giving at Christmas
- the ways in which he shows people from different backgrounds celebrating Christmas.

Keep these notes for revision purposes.

The ghost story genre

Another tradition of the Victorian Christmas was the telling of ghost stories on Christmas Eve. Dickens was well aware of this and *A Christmas Carol* was the first of many successful ghost stories that he wrote. Professor John Mullan on the British Library website says: 'There had been ghosts in literature before the Victorians, but the ghost story as a distinct and popular **genre** was the invention of the Victorians.'

> **convention** an aspect or theme that is common to the genre
>
> **genre** the type of story, such as romance, adventure, horror, ghost story, etc.
>
> **supernatural** something that is beyond nature – seeing the spirit of a dead person, for example

Activity 9

There are a number of **conventions** attached to the ghost story as a genre. Look at those listed below and show how *A Christmas Carol* observes them, using references and quotations as evidence.

a) Weather conditions are foggy and setting is a gloomy, old building.

----

b) Time of day is twilight or night-time.

----

c) The **supernatural** is referred to.

----

d) A story or narrative frames the tale of the ghost(s).

----

e) The protagonist (Scrooge) is established as someone who is real.

Upgrade

It is useful to be able to show how *A Christmas Carol* is part of a tradition of the time, and a Christmas custom. If you can show some knowledge of the conventions of a Victorian ghost story it shows evidence of wider reading.

Victorian London

The story is set in London and Dickens describes different aspects of it throughout the book. In Victorian times it was an overcrowded place, and the main fuel used for heat and cooking was coal, which meant that filthy air was belched from its many chimneys and factories.

 Activity 10

a) Answer the three questions below about each short extract from Stave 1.

i. How does the activity in this quotation convey the thickness of the London fog?

'Meanwhile the fog and darkness thickened so, that people ran about with flaring links*, proffering their services to go before horses in carriages, and conduct them on their way.'

***Links** - torches

----

ii. How does Dickens intensify the feeling of coldness in the underlined phrase?

'The cold became intense. In the main street, at the corner of the court, some labourers were repairing the gas-pipes, and had lighted a great fire in a brazier, round which a party of ragged men and boys were gathered: warming their hands and winking their eyes before the blaze in rapture.'

----

iii. What effect does the image below have on the reader, following the descriptions of the cold and the darkness?

'The brightness of the shops where holly sprigs and berries crackled in the lamp heat of the windows, made pale faces ruddy as they passed.'

----

b) Complete the following activities for the two descriptions from Stave 4 below.

   i. Underline three phrases in the quotation below that show these men are wealthy and explain your choices.

   'They scarcely seemed to enter the city; for the city rather seemed to spring up about them, and encompass them of its own act. But there they were, in the heart of it; on 'Change, amongst the merchants; who hurried up and down, and chinked the money in their pockets, and conversed in groups, and looked at their watches, and trifled thoughtfully with their great gold seals; and so forth, as Scrooge had seen them often.'

   ----

   ii. Write down three phrases in the quotation below that show this is a place of poverty. Explain how Dickens uses the sense of sound and the effect it creates.

   'Far in this den of infamous resort, there was a low-browed, beetling shop, below a pent-house roof, where iron, old rags, bottles, bones, and greasy offal, were bought. Upon the floor within, were piled up heaps of rusty keys, nails, chains, hinges, files, scales, weights, and refuse iron of all kinds. Secrets that few would like to scrutinise were bred and hidden in mountains of unseemly rags, masses of corrupted fat, and sepulchres of bones.'

   ----

   iii. Give your opinion on how and why Dickens could be using a contrast of wealth in these two quotations.

Readers' responses

Context is not only the setting and background of *A Christmas Carol*, but also how readers have responded differently to it at different times.

Activity 11

a) Look at the different views of *A Christmas Carol* below, taken from an article by Michel Faber from *The Guardian*. Put each into the column where you think they belong in the table below, depending on whether you think the quotation displays modern or Victorian views, with a brief reason for your choice. An example has been completed for you. Continue the table on separate paper.

i.

> 'A tale to make the reader laugh and cry – to open his hands, and open his heart to charity even toward the uncharitable...a dainty dish to set before a King.'

ii.

> '*A Christmas Carol*...struck a chord so resounding that it's still instantly recognized by millions of people.'

iii.

> '...a moral story...with not a jot of religion in it'

iv.

> '...if *A Christmas Carol* is less than convincing as a psychological case history of an elderly neurotic temporarily reformed by Christmas sentimentality, it is certainly a success as the metaphysical study of a human being's rediscovery of his own innocence.'

v.

> 'If Christmas, with its ancient and hospitable customs, its social and charitable observances, were ever in danger of decay, this is the book that would give them a new lease.'

vi.

> '*A Christmas Carol* is also very much a scathing social commentary on Dickens's time.'

Victorian	Modern
'A tale to make the reader laugh and cry – to open his hands, and open his heart to charity even toward the uncharitable...a dainty dish to set before a King.' This quotation suggests the social hierarchy in the novella would appeal to a King, which is an old-fashioned viewpoint.	

b) What do you think the views opposite tell us about the readers of the book in two very different times?

Progress check

Use the chart below to review the skills you have developed in this chapter. For each column, start at the bottom box and work your way up towards the highest level in the top box. Tick the box to show you have achieved that level.

Personal response	Textual references	Text and context
I can sustain a critical response to *A Christmas Carol* and interpret the context convincingly ☐	I can use well-integrated textual references from *A Christmas Carol* to support my interpretation ☐	I can show a perceptive understanding of how *A Christmas Carol* is shaped by its context ☐
I can develop a coherent response to *A Christmas Carol* and explain the context clearly ☐	I can use quotations and other textual references from *A Christmas Carol* to support my explanation ☐	I understand the context of *A Christmas Carol* and can make connections between the text and its context ☐
I can make some comments on the context in *A Christmas Carol* ☐	I can make references to some details from *A Christmas Carol* ☐	I am aware of the context in which *A Christmas Carol* was written ☐

Characters

Main characters

Ebenezer Scrooge

Ebenezer Scrooge is the central character in the story, which is built around his conversion from hard **skinflint** into generous **benefactor**.

Activity 1

Look at the three quotations below from Stave 1, which are about the first three things we learn about Scrooge.

What is the reader's first impression of him and why do you think Dickens presents him in this way to begin with?

a)
> 'And Scrooge's name was good upon 'Change, for anything he chose to put his hand to.' *(Stave 1)*

b)
> 'Scrooge was his sole **executor**, his sole **administrator**, his sole **assign**, his sole **residuary legatee**, his sole friend, and sole mourner.' *(Stave 1)*

-------------------------------------   -------------------------------------

-------------------------------------   -------------------------------------

-------------------------------------   -------------------------------------

-------------------------------------   -------------------------------------

c)
> 'And even Scrooge was not so dreadfully cut up by the sad event, but that he was an excellent man of business on the very day of the funeral, and solemnised it with an undoubted bargain.' *(Stave 1)*

----

administrator the person who actually carries out the terms of a will
assign the person to whom the property and affairs of the dead person are transferred
benefactor someone who gives to or benefits others
'Change the Royal Exchange, London's financial centre
executor a person responsible for seeing the terms of a will are carried out
residuary legatee the person who inherits all the estate after bills have been paid
skinflint mean or tight-fisted person

Activity 2

The quotations in Activity 1 were mainly about Scrooge as a businessman. Look at the way Dickens describes his character here and answer the questions that follow.

'External heat and cold had little influence on Scrooge. No warmth could warm, no wintry weather chill him. No wind that blew was bitterer than he, no falling snow was more intent upon its purpose, no pelting rain less open to entreaty.' (Stave 1)

a) How does Dickens use contrasting temperatures to convey Scrooge's lack of humanity?

_____

_____

_____

_____

_____

b) Which three types of weather is Scrooge compared with and what does each of these suggest about him?

_____

_____

_____

_____

_____

_____

c) Find two more quotations where Dickens compares Scrooge with the weather and say what effect is created by each one.

_____

_____

_____

_____

_____

Scrooge's character is also presented through details.

Activity 3

a) Find a quotation in Stave 1 that justifies each statement below.

    i. Scrooge is mean with coal.

----

    ii. Scrooge prefers banking books to the company of others.

----

    iii. Scrooge has a sarcastic sense of humour.

----

b) Write a paragraph on separate paper based on your chosen quotations, showing
how Dickens presents Scrooge's dealings with others through details about his
actions/words.

After the visit by Marley's ghost, Scrooge's character begins to change as he is
visited by three apparitions. The first is the Ghost of Christmas Past.

Activity 4

a) What event prompts each of these comments by Scrooge in Stave 2? Complete the table.

Quotation	Event
"Nothing. There was a boy singing a Christmas Carol at my door last night. I should like to have given him something: that's all."	
"I should like to be able to say a word or two to my clerk just now. That's all."	
"Spirit!" said Scrooge, "show me no more! Conduct me home. Why do you delight to torture me?"	
"Leave me! Take me back. Haunt me no longer!"	

b) On a separate piece of paper, write three paragraphs about how Dickens presents
the changes in Scrooge in Stave 2.

Scrooge is then confronted by the Ghost of Christmas Present in his transformed room.

Activity 5

a) Look at each of the quotations from Stave 3 below and suggest what they tell the reader about Scrooge's state of mind.

i. "I went forth last night on compulsion, and I learnt a lesson which is working now. To-night, if you have aught* to teach me, let me profit by it."

*aught - anything

----

ii. "Spirit," said Scrooge, with an interest he had never felt before, "tell me if Tiny Tim will live."

----

iii. "Scrooge hung his head to hear his own words quoted by the Spirit, and was overcome with penitence and grief."

----

iv. "Scrooge had his eye upon them, and especially on Tiny Tim, until the last."

----

b) Look at each of the underlined phrases above and comment on the language used by Dickens to show Scrooge's changing feelings.

As the ghost dwindles away, the Spirit of Christmas Yet to Come appears and beckons Scrooge to follow it.

Stave 4 is mostly about death and the reactions of people to it.

Activity 6

a) Find three examples of reactions from other people to Scrooge's death in Stave 4, considering what they say, what they do and the effect this has on Scrooge.

Example	Words	Actions	Effect on Scrooge

b) Circle the phrases below you think apply to Scrooge after the spirit shows him his grave.

He is terrified.   He does not care.   He wants a chance to reform.

He just wants to live as before.   He promises to mend his ways.   He does not listen to spirits.

He says he will love Christmas.   He just wants to forget the night.

He will live in past, present and future.

At the start of Stave 5, Scrooge is happy to find himself alive and that he has not missed Christmas Day.

Activity 7

a) Look at the spider diagram and add more boxes showing how Scrooge helps different people. Add one or more quotations to support your ideas.

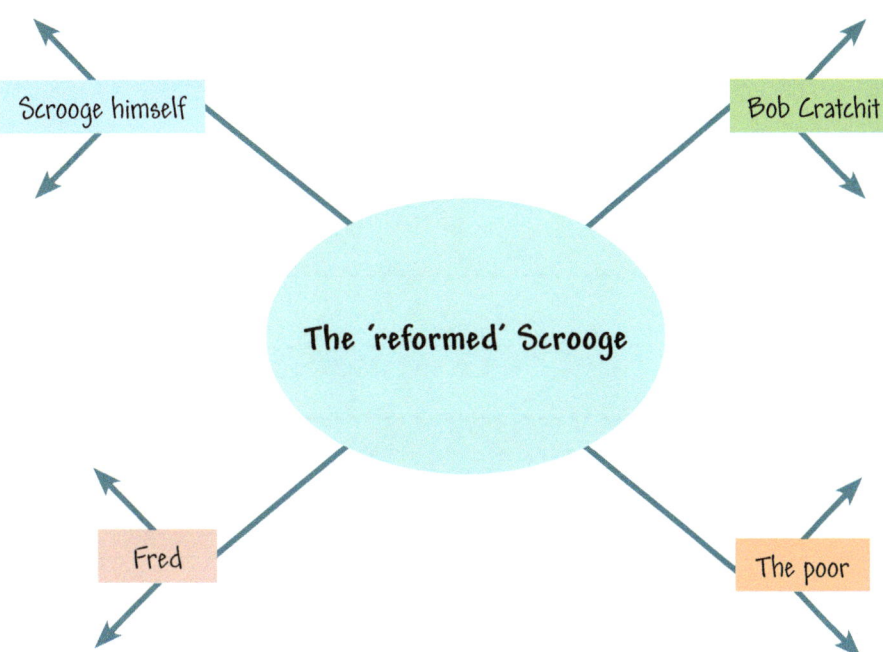

Scrooge himself

Bob Cratchit

The 'reformed' Scrooge

Fred

The poor

b) Read the quotation from Stave 5 below and underline three phrases that show how Dickens presents the reformed Scrooge.

'He dressed himself "all in his best", and at last got out into the streets. The people were by this time pouring forth, as he had seen them with the Ghost of Christmas Present; and walking with his hands behind him, Scrooge regarded every one with a delighted smile. He looked so irresistibly pleasant, in a word, that three or four good-humoured fellows said, "Good morning, sir! A merry Christmas to you!" And Scrooge said often afterwards, that of all the blithe sounds he had ever heard, those were the blithest in his ears.' *(Stave 5)*

Bob Cratchit

Bob Cratchit is Scrooge's clerk and is kept busy writing letters and keeping the accounts up to date. Scrooge has little concern for his comfort and Dickens describes Cratchit's room as a **'sort of tank'**.

 Activity 8

a) Write a list of the words and phrases that Dickens uses about Bob, choosing examples from Staves 1, 3, 4 and 5.

---

b) Comment on how Dickens presents Cratchit in the following instances. For each one, include at least one relevant quotation.

i. In Scrooge's office in Stave 1

---

ii. On Christmas Day in his home in Stave 3

---

iii. After the death of Tiny Tim in Stave 4

---

iv. In Scrooge's office in Stave 5

---

c) Using your answers above, write a paragraph on separate paper describing what you would tell someone who had never read the story about Bob.

Tiny Tim

We first see Tiny Tim being carried on his father's shoulders as they return home from church on Christmas Day.

Activity 9

a) Look at the statements below and decide which are true and which are false.

Tiny Tim is a normal healthy youngster. _____

He wears an iron frame round one leg. _____

His siblings find him a nuisance. _____

His father worries about him. _____

He has a lovely singing voice. _____

He misbehaves in church. _____

His siblings make sure he joins in the fun. _____

Scrooge used to think he should die and decrease the surplus population. _____

He hopes people see him in church and think of Jesus's healing powers. _____

Scrooge hopes he will not die. _____

b) Make a list of the words and phrases Dickens uses to make the reader feel sympathy for Tiny Tim at the Cratchits' Christmas celebration in Stave 3.

_____

_____

_____

_____

c) Why do you think Dickens includes Tiny Tim in the novel:

i. in Stave 3?

_____

_____

ii. in Stave 4?

_____

_____

Fred

Fred is the son of Scrooge's sister, Fanny, and the opposite in character to his uncle.

Activity 10

Read the following paragraph written by a student.

> Fred represents warmth and light and generosity. Unlike his frozen and grasping uncle, he reaches out to people, including the poor and tries to help them. He won't return his uncle's insults, although he does make fun of him. He is not interested in Scrooge's money but wishes the old man would enjoy himself.

a) Although the student makes perceptive comments, there is no evidence to show where the ideas came from. Rewrite this extract from the student's answer including evidence from the text to support these ideas.

----

b) What role does Fred play in the story as a whole? Look at the statements below and number them in order of importance.

He acts as a contrast to Scrooge. `_____`

He shows the true meaning of Christmas. `_____`

He demonstrates how having a good time does not mean forgetting others. `_____`

He offers an example to Scrooge of forgiveness. `_____`

He shows what it means to be among friends and family. `_____`

He teaches Scrooge to join in with others. `_____`

He has a contagious laugh. `_____`

He does not treat Scrooge as Scrooge treats him. `_____`

He is the life and soul of the party. `_____`

Jacob Marley

During his lifetime Jacob Marley was Scrooge's partner and as mean and money-loving as Scrooge. He appears as a ghost to warn Scrooge of what he can expect in the afterlife.

Activity 11

Look at the quotations below from Stave 1 and for each one write down what you think Marley's ghost is specifically warning Scrooge about.

a)
"…if that spirit goes not forth in life, it is condemned to do so after death. It is doomed to wander through the world—oh, woe is me!—and witness what it cannot share, but might have shared on earth, and turned to happiness!"

b)
"Or would you know," pursued the Ghost, "the weight and length of the strong coil you bear yourself? It was full as heavy and as long as this, seven Christmas Eves ago. You have laboured on it, since. It is a ponderous chain!"

c)
"Why did I walk through crowds of fellow-beings with my eyes turned down, and never raise them to that blessed Star which led the Wise Men to a poor abode! Were there no poor homes to which its light would have conducted *me*!"

d)
"I am here to-night to warn you, that you have yet a chance and hope of escaping my fate. A chance and hope of my procuring, Ebenezer."

e)
"Without their visits," said the Ghost, "you cannot hope to shun the path I tread. Expect the first to-morrow, when the bell tolls One."

The Ghost of Christmas Past

The Ghost of Christmas Past reminds Scrooge of his own childhood and youth.

Activity 12

Look at the quotations in the table below from Stave 2 and comment on the impression they give of the Ghost and its lessons for Scrooge.

Quotation	Comment
"The school is not quite deserted," said the Ghost. "A solitary child, neglected by his friends, is left there still."	
'The Ghost smiled thoughtfully, and waved its hand: saying as it did so, "Let us see another Christmas!"'	
"Always a delicate creature, whom a breath might have withered," said the Ghost. "But she had a large heart!"	
"She died a woman," said the Ghost, "and had, as I think, children."	
"A small matter," said the Ghost, "to make these silly folks so full of gratitude."	
'But the relentless Ghost pinioned him in both his arms, and forced him to observe what happened next.'	

The Ghost of Christmas Present

The Ghost of Christmas Present is Scrooge's second visitor, and very different from the first.

Activity 13

Look at the first impression Dickens gives the reader of this second visitor in Stave 3.

In easy state upon this couch, there sat <u>a jolly Giant</u>, glorious to see; who bore <u>a glowing torch</u>, in shape <u>not unlike Plenty's horn</u>, and held it up, high up, to shed its light on Scrooge, as he came peeping round the door.

"Come in!" exclaimed the Ghost. "Come in! and <u>know me better, man!</u>"

Scrooge entered timidly, and hung his head before this Spirit. He was not the dogged Scrooge he had been; and though <u>the Spirit's eyes were clear and kind</u>, he did not like to meet them.

"I am the Ghost of Christmas Present," said the Spirit. "Look upon me!"

Scrooge reverently did so. It was clothed <u>in one simple green robe, or mantle</u>, bordered with white fur. This garment hung so loosely on the figure, that <u>its capacious breast was bare</u>, as if disdaining to be warded or concealed by any artifice. Its feet, observable beneath the ample folds of the garment, were also bare; and on its head it wore no other covering <u>than a holly wreath, set here and there with shining icicles. Its dark brown curls were long and free</u>; free as its <u>genial face</u>, its <u>sparkling eye</u>, its <u>open hand</u>, its <u>cheery voice</u>, its <u>unconstrained demeanour</u>, and <u>its joyful air</u>. Girded round its middle was an antique scabbard; but <u>no sword was in it</u>, and the ancient <u>sheath was eaten up with rust</u>.

How does Dickens present the Ghost of Christmas Present through its physical description? Annotate the underlined phrases above and comment below on what the reader learns about the spirit.

The Ghost of Christmas Yet to Come

The Ghost of Christmas Yet to Come is the final visitor of those promised by Marley.

Activity 14

a) Answer the following questions, providing a reference or quotation as evidence.

   i. How is this ghost different from the previous two?

----

   ii. Why does Dickens present it as silent?

----

   iii. How does Scrooge feel about this spirit?

----

   iv. How does the spirit make its intentions known to Scrooge?

----

   v. How does this spirit reinforce what Marley's ghost said to Scrooge?

----

b) Write a list of words and phrases from Dickens's description of the ghost that suggest it has connections with death and misery.

----

c) Find two phrases near the end of the stave that imply the ghost feels some pity for Scrooge.

Fezziwig

Fezziwig was Scrooge's first employer, to whom he was apprenticed.

Activity 15

a) Complete the table below with three quotations for each of the following.

About Fezziwig	Quotations
What Fezziwig looks like	
What Fezziwig says	
What Fezziwig does	
How others react to Fezziwig	
What the narrator tells us about Fezziwig	
Scrooge's reaction to him	

b) Why do you think Dickens includes Fezziwig in the story?

Belle

Belle was Scrooge's one-time fiancée when he was much younger.

Activity 16

a) Look at this speech by Belle in Stave 2 and write what each of the highlighted phrases tells us about the relationship between Belle and Scrooge.

> "But if you were free to-day, to-morrow, yesterday, can even I believe that you would choose a dowerless girl—you who, in your very confidence with her, weigh everything by Gain: or, choosing her, if for a moment you were false enough to your one guiding principle to do so, do I not know that your repentance and regret would surely follow? I do; and I release you. With a full heart, for the love of him you once were."

b) The ghost insists on showing Scrooge the happiness that Belle found as a wife and mother. How does Dickens contrast her life with Scrooge's?

_____

_____

Activity 17

Dickens is well known for being able to portray a character in only a few words, such as **'In came Mrs. Fezziwig, one vast substantial smile'** _(Stave 2)_.

Look at the characters below and find a brief quotation that gives the reader a good idea of them.

a) Mrs Cratchit _(Stave 3)_

_____

b) Peter Cratchit _(Stave 3)_

_____

c) Martha Cratchit _(Stave 3)_

_____

d) The charity collector _(Stave 1)_

_____

e) Old Joe – the receiver of stolen goods _(Stave 4)_

_____

Upgrade

Remember that when you are asked to write about a character, the examiner will expect you to show why Dickens has included the character and what role he or she plays in the novella. For example, if the question concerns Fred, you would need to examine Fred's character and to explain his part in the story.

Minor characters

The minor characters of *A Christmas Carol* include the other members of the Cratchit family, the thieves who gather round the dead Scrooge, the woman called Caroline and her family (Scrooge's debtors), the charity collectors and numerous others who appear only briefly.

 ## Progress check

Use the chart below to review the skills you have developed in this chapter. For each column, start at the bottom box and work your way up towards the highest level in the top box. Tick the box to show you have achieved that level.

I can sustain a critical response to *A Christmas Carol* and interpret the characterization convincingly ☐	I can use well-integrated textual references from *A Christmas Carol* to support my interpretation ☐	I can analyse the effects of Dickens' use of language, structure and form in *A Christmas Carol*, using subject terms judiciously ☐
I can develop a coherent response to *A Christmas Carol* and explain the characterization clearly ☐	I can use quotations and other textual references from *A Christmas Carol* to support my explanation ☐	I can explain how Dickens uses language, structure and form to create effects in *A Christmas Carol*, using relevant subject terms ☐
I can make some comments on the characterization in *A Christmas Carol* ☐	I can make references to some details from *A Christmas Carol* ☐	I can identify some of Dickens' methods in *A Christmas Carol* and use some subject terms ☐
Personal response	**Textual references**	**Language, structure, form**

Language

Consideration of the way Dickens uses language is very important when studying his writing. He is a master of language use and his techniques are varied.

Humour

One of the ways in which Dickens creates humour is through his digressions i.e. intruding as an author/narrator to make a comment on the story or a character.

Activity 1

a) Look at the following examples of this digression and comment on their humorous effect.

Quotation	Comment
'Mind! I don't mean to say that I know, of my own knowledge, what there is particularly dead about a door-nail.' *(Stave 1)*	
'I should have liked, I do confess, to have had the lightest licence of a child, and yet to have been man enough to know its value.' *(Stave 2)*	
'...as you or I would have thought at first; for it is always the person not in the predicament who knows what ought to have been done in it, and would unquestionably have done it too...' *(Stave 3)*	
'May that be truly said of us, and all of us! And so, as Tiny Tim observed, God bless Us, Every One!' *(Stave 5)*	

b) Why do you think Dickens does not make these digressions in Stave 4?

Other ways in which Dickens creates humorous effects are through wordplay (including **puns** and **inversions**) and absurd comparisons (**simile** and **personification**).

> **inversion** using a phrase that can have more than one meaning
> **personification** a comparison that gives human qualities to inanimate or abstract things
> **pun** a word or phrase that can have more than one meaning
> **simile** a comparison between two things that states one is 'like' or 'as' the other

Activity 2

Match the quotations below with one of these corresponding language terms.

Pun   Inversion   Simile   Personification

Quotation	Literary effect used
'They often "came down" handsomely, and Scrooge never did' *(Of the weather, Stave 1)*	
'Nature lived hard by, and was brewing on a large scale.' *(Stave 1)*	
"you'll keep your Christmas by losing your situation!" *(Stave 1)*	
'like a bad lobster in a dark cellar' *(Stave 1)*	
'…unlike the celebrated herd in the poem, they were not forty children conducting themselves like one, but every child was conducting itself like forty.' *(Stave 2)*	
'whose gruff old bell was always peeping slily down at Scrooge' *(Stave 1)*	
'Scrooge resumed his labours with an improved opinion of himself, and in a more facetious temper than was usual with him.' *(After refusing to help charity, Stave 1)*	
'his mind flew back again, like a strong spring released' *(Stave 2)*	
'and tuned like fifty stomach-aches' *(Stave 2)*	
"There's more of gravy than of grave about you, whatever you are!" *(Stave 1)*	

Upgrade

Although you do not have to identify every language feature in your exam answer, to achieve the higher grades you need to have a sound knowledge of literary terminology and to use it. You will get more marks for saying 'Dickens's use of humorous similes' than for using 'words' or 'phrases'.

Creating a mental picture

Dickens is very good at building up scenes and pictures in the minds of his readers. He uses several language techniques to do this.

Hyperbole

Dickens uses **hyperbole** to expand a scene or image for the reader. Often Dickens's hyperbole takes the form of lists. Sometimes it is a list of **qualifying words** that is extended out, as in the description of Scrooge at the start of the novella, or Fred's description of the qualities of Christmas.

These can be humorous simply because there are so many of them.

> **hyperbole** exaggeration for effect
>
> **qualifying word** a word that describes, such as an adjective or adverb

Activity 3

a) Look at the way Dickens presents Fezziwig's guests in Stave 2. Highlight the words that describe the way the guests entered.

> In they all came, one after another; some shyly, some boldly, some gracefully, some awkwardly, some pushing, some pulling; in they all came, anyhow and everyhow.

b) What effect does Dickens create by using so many adverbs?

----

c) Dickens also uses lists of items, like those forming the throne of the Ghost of Christmas Present, or the window displays in the shops, but not all his lists are for humour.

Highlight the list of items in the following quotation from old Joe's Den in Stave 4.

> Upon the floor within, were piled up heaps of rusty keys, nails, chains, hinges, files, scales, weights, and refuse iron of all kinds.

What is the effect of using a list in this quotation?

----

d) The other kind of list Dickens uses is lists of actions. Look at this account of Belle's husband returning home with presents for the children, from Stave 2. Highlight the verbs Dickens uses in this extract.

> Then the shouting and the struggling, and the onslaught that was made on the defenceless porter! The scaling him with chairs for ladders to dive into his pockets, despoil him of brown-paper parcels, hold on tight by his cravat, hug him round his neck, pommel his back, and kick his legs in irrepressible affection!

How effective do you think he is in showing the children's excitement?

Use of the senses

Activity 4

Highlight how Dickens uses the sense of smell in the following extract from Stave 3 to create tension as the Cratchit family wait for their Christmas pudding.

> "Hallo! A great deal of steam! The pudding was out of the copper. A smell like a washing-day! That was the cloth. A smell like an eating-house and a pastrycook's next door to each other, with a laundress's next door to that! That was the pudding!"

What kind of atmosphere does Dickens create and what effect does this have?

Activity 5

a) Look at the following description of Scrooge's old school in Stave 2. Use different colours to highlight the words and phrases that appeal to different senses. Then annotate them to show which sense is being appealed to and its effect on the reader.

> They left the high-road, by a well-remembered lane, and soon approached a mansion of dull red brick, with a little weathercock-surmounted cupola on the roof, and a bell hanging in it. It was a large house, but one of broken fortunes; for the spacious offices were little used, their walls were damp and mossy, their windows broken, and their gates decayed. Fowls clucked and strutted in the stables; and the coach-houses and sheds were over-run with grass. Nor was it more retentive of its ancient state, within; for entering the dreary hall, and glancing through the open doors of many rooms, they found them poorly furnished, cold, and vast. There was an earthy savour in the air, a chilly bareness in the place, which associated itself somehow with too much getting up by candle-light, and not too much to eat.

b) Find five adjectives or adverbs in the extract above that suggest the place is neglected.

----

c) What impression does Dickens give of the school through appealing to the senses of the reader and also in his choice of adjectives and adverbs? In your answer, include some of your selected words/phrases as evidence for your ideas.

Figures of speech

Dickens also uses other language techniques to build up his mental pictures, such as **imagery**, **connotations** and **metaphor**. Look at an example of each feature in *A Christmas Carol* in the table below.

Language technique	Quotation/Example
Imagery	**'The fog came pouring in at every chink and keyhole'** *(Stave 1)*
Connotations	**'Christmas'** is a word with many connotations, since people associate it with a variety of traditions and customs.
Metaphor	**'The cold within him froze his old features, nipped his pointed nose, shrivelled his cheek, stiffened his gait; made his eyes red, his thin lips blue; and spoke out shrewdly in his grating voice.'** *(Stave 1)*

connotation an image, feeling or idea associated with a word or phrase

imagery using words that create mental images

metaphor the comparison of a thing, idea or action with another (usually imagined) that is similar

Activity 6

a) Look at the quotations in the table below and suggest which figure of speech is being used and why Dickens has chosen it.

Quotation	Figure of speech	Reason for use
'...the fiddler plunged his hot face into a pot of porter' *(Stave 2)*		
'A positive light appeared to issue from Fezziwig's calves. They shone in every part of the dance like moons.' *(Stave 2)*		
"Another idol has displaced me" *(Stave 2)*		
'...dreadful Death, set up thine altar here, and dress it with such terrors as thou hast at thy command: for this is thy dominion!' *(Stave 4)*		
'Walled in by houses; overrun by grass and weeds, the growth of vegetation's death, not life' *(Stave 4)*		
'...monstrous masses of rude stone were cast about, as though it were the burial-place of giants...' *(Stave 3)*		

b) Write a paragraph about the effect of Dickens's use of figures of speech in creating vivid pictures for the reader. Continue on separate paper.

Sound patterns

Another use of language techniques that brings the book alive is sound patterns – **alliteration**, **repetition** and **onomatopoeia**. These help the rhythm of the language in a book that was often read aloud. Dickens himself gave public readings of the book, which were very popular. Look at an example of each feature from Stave 1 of *A Christmas Carol* in the table below.

alliteration the repetition of first letters in words that follow each other

onomatopoeia a word that sounds like the thing or action it represents

repetition the repeating of words or phrases for effect

Language technique	Example from the text
Alliteration	'It swung so softly in the outset that it scarcely made a sound' *(Stave 1)*
Repetition	'...with ghostly spectacles turned up on its ghostly forehead.' *(Stave 1)*
Onomatopoeia	'...with tremulous vibrations afterwards as if its teeth were chattering' *(of the clock striking, Stave 1)*

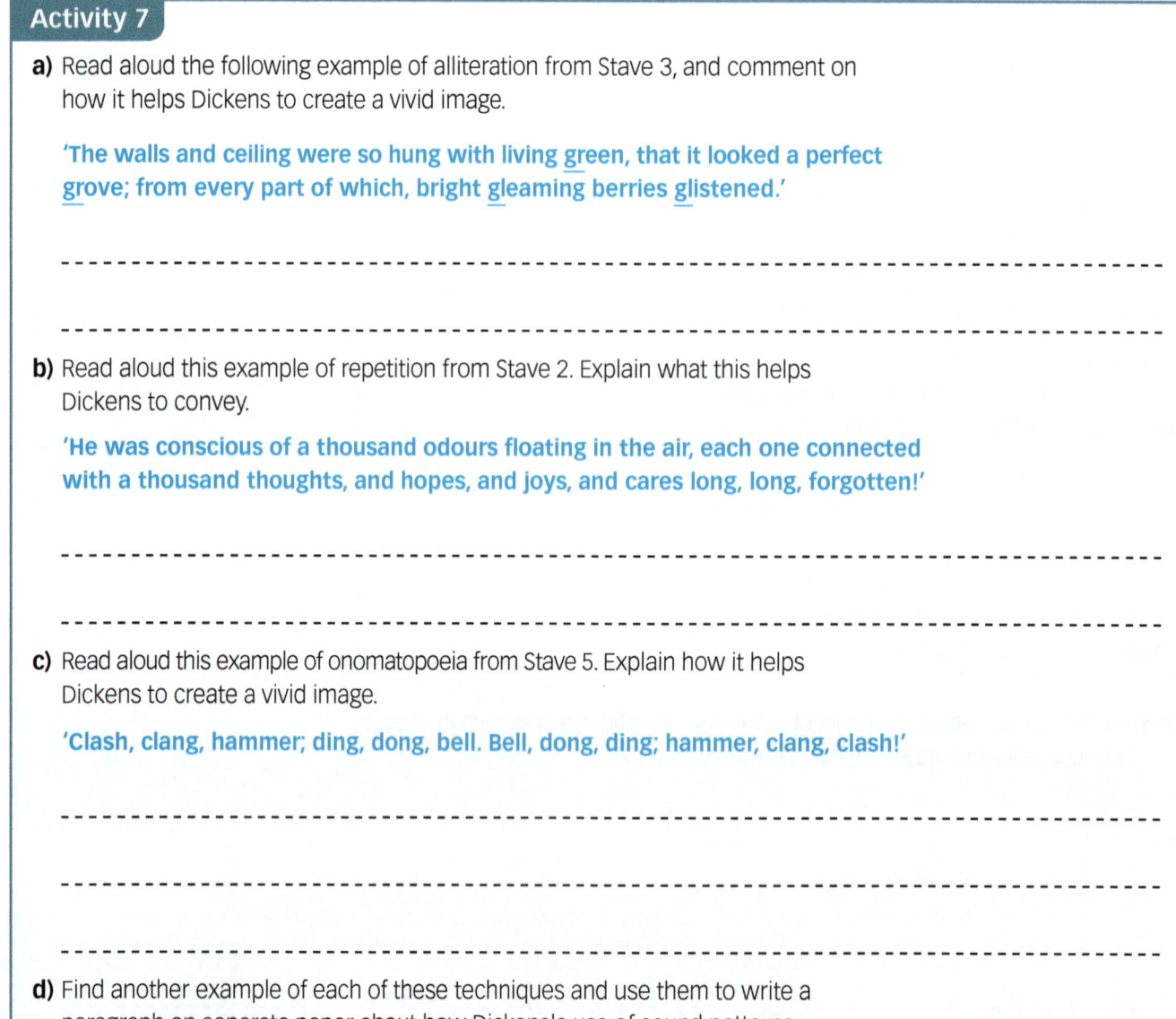

Activity 7

a) Read aloud the following example of alliteration from Stave 3, and comment on how it helps Dickens to create a vivid image.

'The walls and ceiling were so hung with living green, that it looked a perfect grove; from every part of which, bright gleaming berries glistened.'

----

b) Read aloud this example of repetition from Stave 2. Explain what this helps Dickens to convey.

'He was conscious of a thousand odours floating in the air, each one connected with a thousand thoughts, and hopes, and joys, and cares long, long, forgotten!'

----

c) Read aloud this example of onomatopoeia from Stave 5. Explain how it helps Dickens to create a vivid image.

'Clash, clang, hammer; ding, dong, bell. Bell, dong, ding; hammer, clang, clash!'

----

d) Find another example of each of these techniques and use them to write a paragraph on separate paper about how Dickens's use of sound patterns contributes to his imagery.

Dickens' style

In addition to using humour and creating mental pictures, or images, for the reader, Dickens uses a variety of sentence structures that dictate the speed of events at different times. The pace of a story is important to help create an atmosphere, whether it is one of good-natured haste, or slow deliberation.

Activity 8

a) Read the two sentences below that show the actions of two different groups of people and answer the questions that follow.

'But soon the steeples called good people all, to church and chapel, and away they came, flocking through the streets in their best clothes, and with their gayest faces. And at the same time there emerged from scores of bye-streets, lanes, and nameless turnings, innumerable people, carrying their dinners to the bakers' shops.' *(Stave 3)*

i. How does Dickens suggest the streets were full of people?

---

ii. How does he imply that the two lots of people were different?

---

iii. How do the two sentences show a balance between the two groups? Consider sentence length, use of verbs and the descriptions in relation to the streets and the people.

---

b) Read aloud the sentence below and give your views about how Dickens presents the activity that precedes Christmas dinner.

'Mrs. Cratchit made the gravy (ready beforehand in a little saucepan) hissing hot; Master Peter mashed the potatoes with incredible vigour; Miss Belinda sweetened up the apple-sauce; Martha dusted the hot plates; Bob took Tiny Tim beside him in a tiny corner at the table; the two young Cratchits set chairs for everybody, not forgetting themselves, and mounting guard upon their posts, crammed spoons into their mouths, lest they should shriek for goose before their turn came to be helped.' *(Stave 3)*

---

c) Dickens frequently uses short sentences for effect. Find each of the following
short sentences in the text and comment on why you think they are effective.

Sentence	Comment
'Old Marley was as dead as a door-nail.' *(Stave 1)*	
'The city had entirely vanished.' *(Stave 2)*	
'It gave him no reply.' *(Stave 4)*	
'It *was* a Turkey!' *(Stave 5)*	

d) Dickens also uses balanced sentences to give equal weight to two ideas.
Look at the examples below. Identify the division in the sentences and comment
on the two ideas within it. Give your views on why Dickens chose to use it.

"Let me hear another sound from *you*," said Scrooge, "and you'll keep your
Christmas by losing your situation!"

- -

- -

"This lunatic, in letting Scrooge's nephew out, had let two other people in."

- -

- -

"I girded it on of my own free will, and of my own free will I wore it."

- -

- -

"He frightened every one away from him when he was alive, to profit us
when he was dead!"

- -

- -

Dialogue

The way characters speak can tell us about them and their relationships with others. When you imagine a character, you think of how they look and what they do, but you also think of how they speak – or if they speak at all, as in the case of the Ghost of Christmas Yet to Come.

A person's spoken language consists of the vocabulary they use, their accent and the speech mannerisms they may have. Think of Scrooge's famous "Bah! Humbug!" when Christmas is mentioned.

Activity 9

One of the ways in which Dickens shows Scrooge changing through the story is in his use of dialogue. Look at the quotations below and suggest which Stave they come from. Justify your reason.

a)
"Why show me this, if I am past all hope!"

b)
"A great many back-payments are included in it, I assure you."

c)
"Here is a new game," said Scrooge. "One half hour, Spirit, only one!"

d)
"Much good may it do you! Much good it has ever done you!"

e)
"The happiness he gives, is quite as great as if it cost a fortune."

Other characters do not change, like Scrooge, but are still recognizable from their speech.

Activity 10

Can you identify the following characters from what they say? Choose from Fred, Little Fan, Joe, Mrs Cratchit, Fezziwig.

"...but first, we're to be together all the Christmas long, and have the merriest time in all the world." ----------------

"Clear away, my lads, and let's have lots of room here!" ----------------

"I'd give him a piece of my mind to feast upon, and I hope he'd have a good appetite for it." ----------------

"However, his offences carry their own punishment, and I have nothing to say against him." ----------------

"I wouldn't give another sixpence, if I was to be boiled for not doing it." ----------------

Satire and irony

Satire

The use of ridicule to expose the failings of people or institutions is a technique Dickens uses often. Sometimes it is humorous, but it can be harsh. One example is shown at the start of *A Christmas Carol* when Dickens comments: **'And even Scrooge was not so dreadfully cut up by the sad event, but that he was an excellent man of business on the very day of the funeral, and solemnised it with an undoubted bargain.'** *(Stave 1)*

Activity 11

Read on in Stave 1 to find an example of Dickens using satire in relation to Scrooge's behaviour in the roles in the table below. Explain the satire for each example you choose. Continue your table on seperate paper.

Scrooge as an employer	Scrooge as a relative	Scrooge as a philanthropist (supporter of a charity)

While Dickens reserves his harshest satire for the wealthy, like Scrooge, who ignore the sufferings of the poor, he uses a gentle and tolerant satire for others, like the Cratchits such as: **'Such a bustle ensued that you might have thought a goose the rarest of all birds; a feathered phenomenon, to which a black swan was a matter of course—and in truth it was something very like it in that house.'** *(Stave 3)*

This satirizes the undue excitement felt over an ordinary meal, with the intention of showing the reader how low wages affected families.

Activity 12

a) Find an example of satire from each of the following events and comment on how and why Dickens uses it.

i. The phantoms Scrooge sees outside his window after Marley's visitation.

----

ii. Fezziwig's Christmas party

----

iii. Belle's children greeting their father

----

iv. Fred's Christmas party

----

v. The gathering at Joe's slum

----

vi. Scrooge's reaction to finding it is still Christmas Day

----

b) On separate paper, write a set of notes or bullet points on how and why Dickens uses satire in *A Christmas Carol*.

Irony

Dickens often uses irony as part of his satire, in the form of verbal irony, situational irony or dramatic irony.

Verbal irony is saying something when you mean the opposite, like "Oh, well done" to someone who has just dropped something.

Situational irony is when something happens that is opposite to what was intended, like when a new bypass causes traffic congestion somewhere else.

Dramatic irony is when the audience, or readers, know something the characters do not, as when we realize the person being discussed in Stave 4 is Scrooge but he does not.

Activity 13

a) Look at the following examples of irony and decide whether each one is verbal, situational or dramatic irony.

Example	Type of irony
"It should be Christmas Day, I am sure," said she, "on which one drinks the health of such an odious, stingy, hard, unfeeling man as Mr. Scrooge." *(Mrs Cratchit, Stave 3)*	
"What then? If he be like to die, he had better do it, and decrease the surplus population." *(The Ghost of Christmas Present, Stave 3)*	
'…forgetting in the interest he had in what was going on, that his voice made no sound in their ears, he sometimes came out with his guess quite loud, and very often guessed quite right, too' *(Scrooge with the Ghost of Christmas Present at Fred's party, Stave 3)*	
'He thought, if this man could be raised up now, what would be his foremost thoughts? Avarice, hard-dealing, griping cares? They have brought him to a rich end, truly!' *(Seeing the corpse on the bed, Stave 4)*	
"A small matter," said the Ghost, "to make these silly folks so full of gratitude." *(The Ghost of Christmas Past, Stave 2)*	
'Now, being prepared for almost anything, he was not by any means prepared for nothing…' *(Waiting for second spirit, Stave 3)*	

b) On a separate piece of paper, draw a spider diagram of Dickens's use of irony in Stave 4 when he overhears his death being discussed without realizing it.

Symbolism

A Christmas Carol in itself is symbolic, like a fairy tale. Dickens even uses the words 'Once upon a time…' in Stave 1. The main thread of the story concerns redemption, which gives it the moral dimension of a **parable**.

parable a story that shows a moral or spiritual lesson

Activity 14

a) Below are some of the elements often found in fairy tales. Comment on how Dickens uses them in his story and provide a short quotation to support your idea.

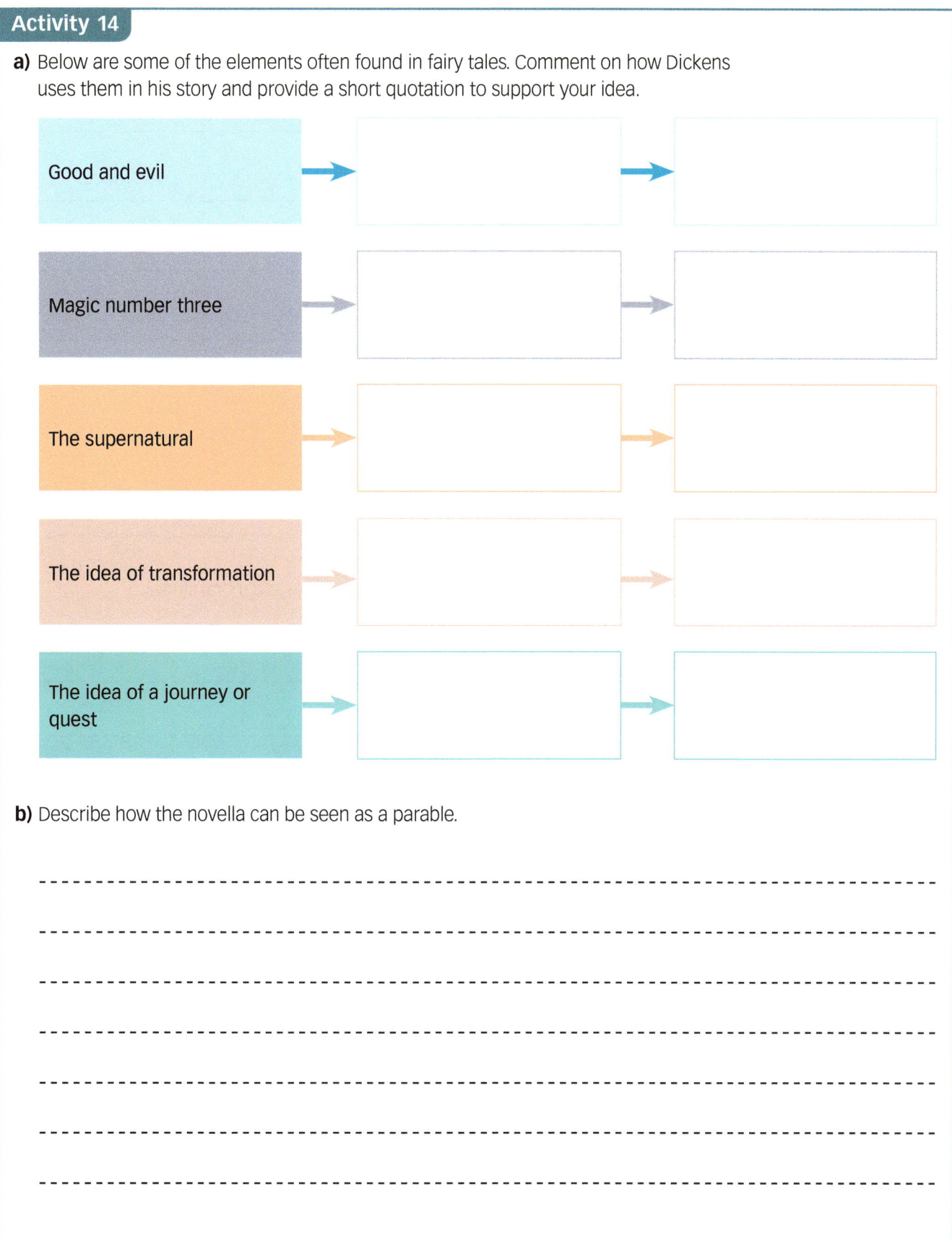

Good and evil		
Magic number three		
The supernatural		
The idea of transformation		
The idea of a journey or quest		

b) Describe how the novella can be seen as a parable.

An **allegory** is a story that has a hidden or less obvious meaning beneath the surface story. It uses characters that represent a type or quality; it presents vices or virtues as characters and uses events that stand for metaphorical or spiritual themes.

> **allegory** a metaphorical story

 Activity 15

How could the following be seen as allegorical?

A Christmas Carol	Allegorical element
The three spirits	
The two children, Want and Ignorance	
Scrooge's journeys with the Ghost of Christmas Present	
The characters of Scrooge and Fred	
The figure of Tiny Tim	

Other symbols are used by Dickens to represent various ideas or qualities in the novella. One of the most important is the weather.

 Activity 16

a) What do the following suggest to the reader about Scrooge and his emotional and moral state?

   i. 'The cold within him froze his old features...' *(Stave 1)*

   ----

   ii. 'The fog came pouring in at every chink and keyhole...' *(Stave 1)*

   ----

   iii. 'Golden sunlight; Heavenly sky; sweet fresh air...' *(Stave 5)*

   ----

b) What do the following symbols represent?

   i. 'it was made...of cash-boxes, keys, padlocks, ledgers, deeds, and heavy purses wrought in steel.' *(Marley's chain, Stave 1)*

   ----

ii. '...like a child: yet not so like a child as like an old man...' *(The Ghost of Christmas Past, Stave 2)*

----

iii. '...a glowing torch, in shape not unlike Plenty's horn...' *(The Ghost of Christmas Present, Stave 3)*

----

iv. '...overrun by grass and weeds, the growth of vegetation's death, not life...'
(Scrooge's grave, Stave 4)

Progress check

Use the chart below to review the skills you have developed in this chapter.
For each column, start at the bottom box and work your way up towards the
highest level in the top box. Tick the box to show you have achieved that level.

I can sustain a critical response to *A Christmas Carol* and interpret the language convincingly ☐	I can use well-integrated textual references from *A Christmas Carol* to support my interpretation ☐	I can analyse the effects of Dickens' use of language, structure and form in *A Christmas Carol*, using subject terms judiciously ☐	I use a wide range of vocabulary and can spell and punctuate consistently accurately ☐
I can develop a coherent response to *A Christmas Carol* and explain the language clearly ☐	I can use quotations and other textual references from *A Christmas Carol* to support my explanation ☐	I can explain how Dickens uses language, structure and form to create effects in *A Christmas Carol*, using relevant subject terms ☐	I use a range of vocabulary and can spell and punctuate, mostly accurately ☐
I can make some comments on the language in *A Christmas Carol* ☐	I can make references to some details from *A Christmas Carol* ☐	I can identify some of Dickens' methods in *A Christmas Carol* and use some subject terms ☐	I use a simple range of vocabulary and spell and punctuate with some accuracy ☐
Personal response	**Textual references**	**Language, structure, form**	**Technical accuracy**

Themes

Poverty and wealth

In Victorian times there was no system of state aid for the poor or those who could not work, other than the workhouse.

Activity 1

Look at the section of Stave 1 where the charity collectors visit Scrooge's office. Then answer the following questions.

a) Why are the charity collectors asking for money?

----

b) Prisons were harsh places where men and women were separated and made to work hard for minimal food and comfort. What does it tell us about Scrooge that he thought these places were adequate for the poor?

----

c) What does Scrooge suggest the poor should do if they cannot face the hardships in these places?

----

d) What do you think Dickens wants his readers to feel when they read this conversation?

----

e) Why do the charity collectors say it is particularly desirable to help provide for those in need at Christmas?

Dickens show us different levels of wealth and poverty in his story.

Activity 2

Look at the following characters and rank them in order from wealthiest to poorest with 7 as the best off and 1 as the poorest.

Scrooge's nephew, Fred _____

The Cratchit family _____

Scrooge and his associates _____

The children under the robes of the Ghost of Christmas Present _____

Caroline and her family in Stave 4 _____

Fezziwig _____

Joe, the receiver of stolen goods _____

Dickens makes a distinction between poverty and destitution (extreme poverty or need that could be fatal). Although the Cratchit family is poor, the figures of Want and Ignorance are in a different class.

Activity 3

Read the extract from Stave 3 below and answer the questions that follow.

> They were a boy and a girl. Yellow, meagre, ragged, scowling, wolfish; but prostrate, too, in their humility. Where graceful youth should have filled their features out, and touched them with its freshest tints, a stale and shrivelled hand, like that of age, had pinched, and twisted them, and pulled them into shreds. Where angels might have sat enthroned, devils lurked, and glared out menacing. No change, no degradation, no perversion of humanity, in any grade, through all the mysteries of wonderful creation, has monsters half so horrible and dread.
>
> Scrooge started back, appalled. Having them shown to him in this way, he tried to say they were fine children, but the words choked themselves, rather than be parties to a lie of such enormous magnitude.

a) Look at the first three sentences of this quotation. Annotate and comment below on the way that Dickens uses contrast to make the children appear even more wretched.

----

b) Look at the fourth sentence and comment on how Dickens builds up the shocking state of the children through repetition and hyperbole.

----

c) Look at the final sentence of the quotation and give your views on how Dickens completes the picture of Want and Ignorance through Scrooge's reactions.

Greed and generosity

In his depiction of greed and generosity, Dickens does not only include money and goods but also the giving or withholding of a person's thoughts and feelings. The novel starts with Scrooge's chilled emotions and the surrounding fog that blinds him morally.

Activity 4

a) Look at the quotations below and tick the heading that applies.

Quotation	Greed	Generosity
'To edge his way along the crowded paths of life, warning all human sympathy to keep its distance...' (Of Scrooge, Stave 1)		
"...a few of us are endeavouring to raise a fund to buy the Poor some meat and drink, and means of warmth." (Charity collector, Stave 1)		
"The happiness he gives, is quite as great as if it cost a fortune." (Scrooge, of Fezziwig, Stave 2)		
'The Spirit stood beside sick beds, and they were cheerful; on foreign lands, and they were close at home; by struggling men, and they were patient in their greater hope; by poverty, and it was rich.' (The Ghost of Christmas Present, Stave 3)		
"Putting it on him to be buried in, to be sure," replied the woman with a laugh. "Somebody was fool enough to do it, but I took it off again." (Charwoman, Stave 4)		
"If I can be of service to you in any way," he said, giving me his card, "that's where I live. Pray come to me." (Bob, of Fred, Stave 4)		
"I'll send it to Bob Cratchit's!" whispered Scrooge, rubbing his hands, and splitting with a laugh. "He sha'n't know who sends it. It's twice the size of Tiny Tim." (Scrooge, Stave 5)		

b) What do you think these examples show about the way Dickens presents ideas of greed and generosity?

Dickens shows that, despite his behaviour, deep inside Scrooge knows the meaning of generosity. The importance of memory in unlocking this comes with the Ghost of Christmas Past.

Activity 5

a) Comment on how each of the following characters contribute to Scrooge's realization of missed opportunities for generosity.

i. His sister, 'little Fan'

----

ii. His first employer, Fezziwig

----

iii. His ex-fiancée, Belle

----

b) Dickens uses the Ghost of Christmas Present to show Scrooge many examples of Christmas celebration and giving. What do these examples have in common?

----

c) The Ghost of Christmas Yet to Come shows different forms of greed and generosity.

i. Find three different examples of greed in Stave 4.

----

ii. Find two different examples of generosity in Stave 4.

----

iii. How and why are the examples Dickens presents in this stave different from the examples in Staves 2 and 3?

Time and space

Dickens shows the three Christmas ghosts being able to operate outside time and space. In one night Scrooge experiences a whole lifetime and from one room he visits different parts of his city, his country and beyond.

Activity 6

Complete the spider diagram below with examples and/or quotations of Scrooge's experiences.

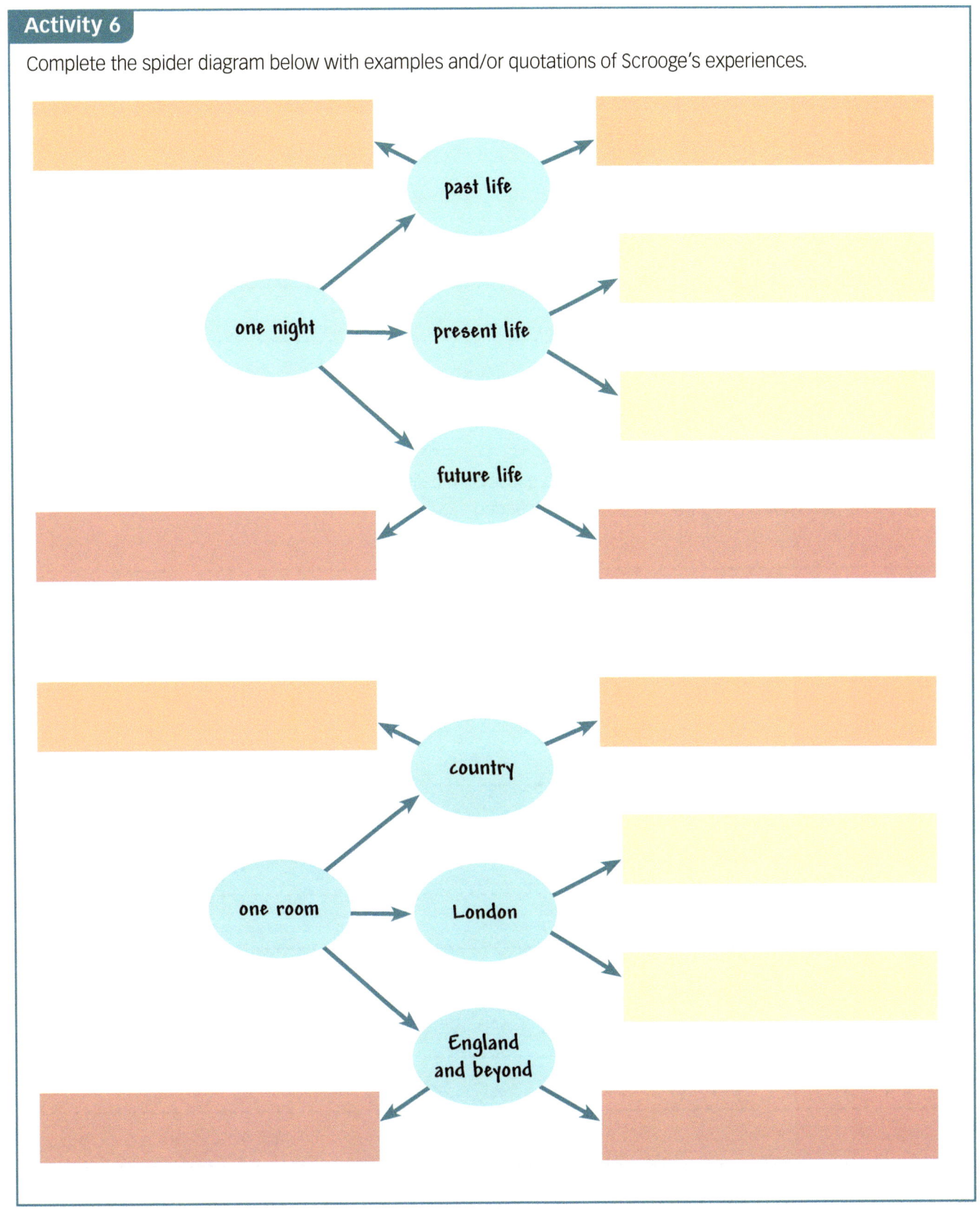

Dickens shows each of the ghosts appearing as the clock strikes – yet they all visit Scrooge in the same night.

Activity 7

a) How does Dickens present the ghosts' ability to move from one event to another with Scrooge, without seeming to travel in time or space? Give examples.

----

b) Dickens needed to find a way to make Scrooge's conversion believable in a single night. Give your view on whether and how he succeeded.

Light and dark

Dickens uses imagery that shows light/heat and dark/cold related to emotional, moral, and physical states.

Activity 8

a) What is Dickens using light/heat to symbolize in the following quotations?

i.
> '...had lighted a great fire in a brazier, round which a party of ragged men and boys were gathered...' (*Stave 1*)

----

ii.
> '...a cheerful company assembled round a glowing fire.' (*Stave 3*)

----

iii.
> 'Then all the Cratchit family drew round the hearth, in what Bob Cratchit called a circle...' (*Stave 3*)

----

iv.
> 'But even here, two men who watched the light had made a fire, that through the loophole in the thick stone wall shed out a ray of brightness on the awful sea.' (*Stave 3*)

----

b) What does Scrooge's comment below indicate to the reader?

> "Make up the fires, and buy another coal-scuttle before you dot another i, Bob Cratchit!" (*Stave 5*)

Welcoming light and fearing darkness are things deep in the human mind, so that Scrooge's welcoming of the dark signals to readers that he is unnatural. **'The yard was so dark that even Scrooge, who knew its every stone, was fain to grope with his hands. The fog and frost so hung about the black old gateway of the house…'** *(Stave 1)*

Activity 9

a) What is Dickens suggesting by his use of darkness and shadows in the following quotations?

Quotation	What it suggests
'…but it was quite dark already—it had not been light all day…' *(Stave 1)*	
'There was an eager, greedy, restless motion in the eye, which showed the passion that had taken root, and where the shadow of the growing tree would fall.' *(Stave 2)*	
'It was shrouded in a deep black garment, which concealed its head, its face, its form, and left nothing of it visible save one outstretched hand. But for this it would have been difficult to detach its figure from the night, and separate it from the darkness by which it was surrounded.' *(Stave 4)*	
'…an obscure part of the town, where Scrooge had never penetrated before' *(Stave 4)*	
"…the shadows of the things that would have been, may be dispelled. They will be. I know they will!" *(Stave 5)*	

b) In the following quotations, Dickens uses a contrast between light and dark. Annotate the language in each pair of quotations and write what you think this contrast implies.

i.

> 'The sky was gloomy, and the shortest streets were choked up with a dingy mist, half thawed, half frozen, whose heavier particles descended in a shower of sooty atoms' *(Stave 3)*

> '…the fruiterers' were radiant in their glory.' *(Stave 3)*

----

ii.

> '…he seized the extinguisher-cap, and by a sudden action pressed it down upon its head.' *(Stave 2)*

> '…he could not hide the light, which streamed from under it, in an unbroken flood upon the ground.' *(Stave 2)*

----

iii.

> 'The room was very dark, too dark to be observed with any accuracy…' *(Stave 4)*

> '…the warehouse was as snug, and warm, and dry, and bright a ball-room, as you would desire to see upon a winter's night.' *(Stave 2)*

Dickens does not always use light in the same way. It can be warm and welcoming, but it can also seem dazzling, angry, menacing or cold and pale.

 Activity 10

Annotate each of the following quotations to show what use of light Dickens has in mind, and why you think this.

> A positive light appeared to issue from Fezziwig's calves. They shone in every part of the dance like moons.
>
> *(Stave 2)*

> Down in the west the setting sun had left a streak of fiery red, which glared upon the desolation for an instant, like a sullen eye, and frowning lower, lower, lower yet, was lost in the thick gloom of darkest night.
>
> *(Stave 3)*

> A pale light, rising in the outer air, fell straight upon the bed; and on it, plundered and bereft, unwatched, unwept, uncared for, was the body of this man.
>
> *(Stave 4)*

Upgrade

When writing about the themes of a novel it is important to show not only that you understand what they are, but also the techniques Dickens uses to show them and what their effect is on the reader. He uses light to suggest the cheerfulness of Christmas, but also how it illuminates people's thinking and, when combined with warmth, their emotions. The light that memory shines on the past has an effect on the way Scrooge behaves in the present. It chases away the darkness of moral blindness and releases the experience of human love and kindness.

Youth and age

Children had varying experiences of childhood in Victorian times, many of which are displayed by Dickens in *A Christmas Carol*.

Activity 11

Complete this timeline for Scrooge's life. You should include the events that had the most effect on him, such as being left in school at Christmas.

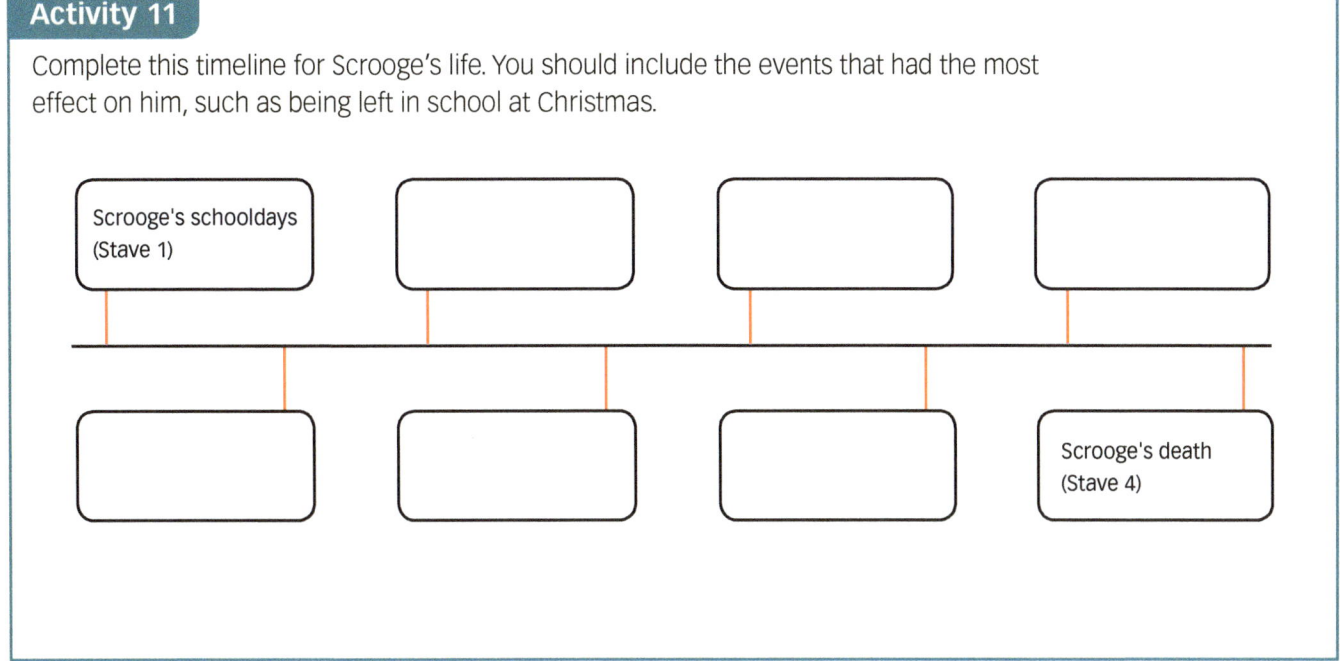

The contrast between age and youth is summed up in the Ghost of Christmas Past, who is both old and young, winter and spring, light and dark. His light burns brightly or dimly according to the clarity of a memory and he resists Scrooge's urge to snuff him out.

Activity 12

Dickens's idea of youthfulness is not merely chronological – it also covers those who are able to connect with their inner child. Find an example of each of the following behaving in a childlike manner.

Character	Example
Bob Cratchit (Stave 1)	
Fezziwig (Stave 2)	
Fred (Stave 3)	
Scrooge (Stave 5)	

Christmas and winter

Christmas celebrations differed according to people's incomes and tastes.

Activity 13

a) How did Scrooge spend Christmas Eve before the ghost of Marley intervened?

----

b) What did Christmas mean to the sailors on the ship visited by Scrooge with the Ghost of Christmas Present?

----

c) How did the Cratchits cook both their goose and their pudding without a kitchen stove or oven?

----

d) What form of music and games were shown at the following?

   i. Belle's family home

----

   ii. The Cratchits

----

   iii. The miner's family in Stave 3

----

   iv. The Fezziwigs' party

----

e) Scrooge is shown three different Christmases by the Ghosts of Past, Present and Future. How are the first two visits different from the final one?

In Dickens's time the winters were severe, usually with heavy snowfalls. For the poor, with little nutrition and inadequate clothing, it meant dreadful hardship and many deaths. This made a winter festival an even more welcome event, especially one that encouraged the better-off to help those in poverty.

Activity 14

The cold is shown in different ways: as an enemy or as pleasant in its own way; as an opportunity for fun or as making people feel alive. Give your own opinion on how Dickens contrasts these varying views for each of the following quotations about cold weather below.

a) 'The owner of one scant young nose, gnawed and mumbled by the hungry cold as bones are gnawed by dogs, stooped down at Scrooge's keyhole to regale him with a Christmas carol' *(Stave 1)*

- -

- -

- -

b) 'The darkness and the mist had vanished with it, for it was a clear, cold, winter day, with snow upon the ground.' *(Stave 2)*

- -

- -

- -

c) "So I am told," returned the second. "Cold, isn't it?" *(Stave 4)*

- -

- -

- -

d) "Seasonable for Christmas time. You're not a skater, I suppose?" *(Stave 4)*

- -

- -

- -

e) 'clear, bright, jovial, stirring, cold; cold, piping for the blood to dance to…' *(Stave 5)*

- -

- -

- -

Families

The importance of family life, especially at Christmas, is presented by Dickens through several family groups. The most important of these is the Cratchit family and Scrooge observes them over two very different Christmases in Stave 3 and Stave 4.

Activity 15

a) Read the two contrasting scenes of Christmas in the Cratchit household in Staves 3 and 4 and compare the following aspects.

	Christmas Present (Stave 3)	Christmas Future (Stave 4)
The general atmosphere of the house		
The relationship between Bob and Tiny Tim		
The actions of the older siblings (Peter, Martha, Belinda)		
The actions of the two younger Cratchits		
The conversation between Bob and Mrs Cratchit		

b) Why do you think Dickens shows Scrooge, and the reader, these two contrasting Christmas scenes?

In Stave 2 Dickens uses the Ghost of Christmas Past to show three very different family Christmases.

Activity 16

a) Find three short references and/or quotations that express each of the following.

   i. The lonely holiday of Ebenezer Scrooge as a boy

----

   ii. The warmth and good fellowship of the Fezziwigs

----

   iii. The affectionate excitement of Belle's children

----

b) In your opinion, why did Dickens include these scenes?

Upgrade

Even if you are not specifically asked about a theme, you could gain marks for including knowledge of how Dickens presents one of them (for example, for writing something about the theme of generosity if you are asked about Fred's character and what it contributes to the novella).

You should also consider any development of themes as the narrative continues, for example, whether we see more generosity at the end of the story than the beginning, or if the display of poverty increases or changes as we read further in the novella.

For Dickens it mattered that families gathered together and had strong bonds.

Activity 17

Look at the following quotations and suggest what Dickens wanted his readers to think.

a)
> "I don't make merry myself at Christmas and I can't afford to make idle people merry." (*Stave 1*)

----

c)
> '...there he was, alone again, when all the other boys had gone home for the jolly holidays.' (*Stave 2*)

----

b)
> "A solitary child, neglected by his friends, is left there still." (*Stave 2*)

----

d)
> "His partner lies upon the point of death, I hear; and there he sat alone." (*Stave 2*)

In contrast to Scrooge's unwanted lonely Christmases as a boy, Dickens presents other families with different attitudes.

Activity 18

a) For each family in the table below, find two quotations: one to show the relationship between the parents, and one to show the relationship between the parents and children.

Family group	Relationship between parents	Relationship between parents and children
Belle's family		
Cratchit family		
Fezziwig family		

b) How do these relationships differ from those in Scrooge's own family?

⊕ Progress check

Use the chart below to review the skills you have developed in this chapter.
For each column, start at the bottom box and work your way up towards the
highest level in the top box. Tick the box to show you have achieved that level.

I can sustain a critical response to *A Christmas Carol* and interpret the themes convincingly ☐	I can use well-integrated textual references from *A Christmas Carol* to support my interpretation ☐	I can show a perceptive understanding of how *A Christmas Carol* is shaped by its context ☐
I can develop a coherent response to *A Christmas Carol* and explain the themes clearly ☐	I can use quotations and other textual references from *A Christmas Carol* to support my explanation ☐	I understand the context of *A Christmas Carol* and can make connections between the text and its context ☐
I can make some comments on the themes in *A Christmas Carol* ☐	I can make references to some details from *A Christmas Carol* ☐	I am aware of the context in which *A Christmas Carol* was written ☐
Personal response	**Textual references**	**Text and context**

Understanding the question

Exam questions include certain words and phrases that should tell you what the examiner wants you to do.

Explore

'Explore' means to look at every aspect of something. Ask the questions, 'What?', 'Where?', 'When?', 'Who?', 'Why?' and 'How?'

Activity 1

Look at the example exam question and complete the table that follows. The first row has been done for you.

> Explore how poverty is shown in *A Christmas Carol*.

Aspect	Examples	Reference/quotation
How poverty is shown?	Through characters such as the Cratchits, Want and Ignorance, the thieves from Scrooge's deathbed.	The Cratchits can only afford a small Christmas dinner. Want and Ignorance are feral children and dangerous. The thieves will steal from the dead – morally low.
Why poverty is shown?		
What kinds of poverty are shown?		
When does Scrooge respond to poverty?		
Who is affected by poverty?		
Why are people in poverty?		

This kind of question will also expect you to show your knowledge of context – in this case the situation of poor people in Victorian England.

How does the author... or Show how the writer...

Questions that begin 'How does the author...' or 'Show how the writer...' mean you will be expected to discuss the writer's techniques, not just what they say, but how they say it. The key word is 'How?'. This is where you can show your knowledge of literary terms.

Activity 2

Test yourself on the techniques below by giving a definition and example for each one.

a) Language use

----

b) Structure

----

c) Imagery

----

d) Metaphor

----

e) Satire

----

f) Irony

----

g) Tension

Present and portray

'Present' and 'portray' mean similar things: how someone or something is written about in the novella. For example, 'How is childhood presented/portrayed in *A Christmas Carol*?'

Activity 3

Write down five views of childhood that Dickens shows in *A Christmas Carol* in the first column. For each view, write a relevant reference or quotation in the second column.

Views of childhood	Reference/quotation

In what ways…

'In what way(s)…' means to look at different angles on something. For example, 'In what ways do the three Christmas ghosts bring about Scrooge's reform?'

Activity 4

For each of the three ghosts, write down two different methods they use to reform Scrooge.

Ghost	Methods of reform
Christmas Past	
Christmas Present	
Christmas Future	

How far...

'How far' means the extent of something. For example, 'How far is Christmas giving important to the story?' You may consider this to be the main theme of the story, so you will need to argue this and support it with evidence.

Activity 5

a) You could approach the question of 'How far is Christmas giving important to the story?' by looking at examples of those who give and those who do not. Copy the table header below on separate paper and write four examples under each heading.

Examples of Christmas giving	Examples of lack of Christmas giving

b) In one sentence describe how important Christmas giving is to *A Christmas Carol* in your opinion.

- -

What role...

'What role...' means you should write about a character and their function in the novel. For example, 'What role does the ghost of Jacob Marley play in the novel?'

Activity 6

To answer the question of 'What role does the ghost of Jacob Marley play in the novel?' you need to think about the function of Marley's ghost and what he does that nothing else would have been able to do. To help with this, answer the questions below.

a) What did Marley have in common with Scrooge that might make Scrooge listen to him?

- -

b) How does Marley's entrance to Scrooge's room make an impression on his former partner?

- -

c) What does Marley's ghost tell Scrooge about the chain he wears and what does he suggest about the one Scrooge is preparing for himself?

- -

- -

d) What does the ghost say his current existence is like and why it is so?

- -

- -

e) What does Marley's ghost tell Scrooge he has done for him as a favour to a friend?

- -

- -

Explain or comment on...

'Explain' or 'comment on...' means you should give your own response in as much detail as you can. For example, 'Explain how Dickens portrays ideas about time and space in *A Christmas Carol*.'

In your answer you would need to show how Dickens takes Scrooge through a whole lifetime in a single night, and how he covers much of London and beyond, from his own bedroom.

Activity 7

a) Complete the table below to consider how Dickens describes the mode of travel of each ghost and where each one takes Scrooge.

Ghost	Description of mode of travel	Different destinations
Christmas Past		
Christmas Present		
Christmas Future		

b) In your opinion, how effective are the journeys made by each of the ghosts in helping Scrooge to reform?

Summary of understanding the question

Activity 8

Based on what you have learned in the previous activities, write down what each of these exam questions is expecting you to do.

a) Explore the way Christmas is presented in the novel.

----

b) Show how Dickens uses suspense in the approach of the four ghosts.

----

c) How is the Cratchit family presented in the novel?

----

d) In what ways does Dickens portray Scrooge's selfishness?

----

e) How far is the manner of someone's death significant in the novel?

----

f) What role is played by Tiny Tim in the novel?

----

g) Comment on the way Scrooge behaves after the ghosts' visits.

Planning your answer

It is always wise to take five minutes at the start of the exam to plan your answer. You can do this in note form, as bullet points or as a spider diagram – whichever method you prefer.

Look at the example exam question below.

> In what ways do the three Christmas ghosts bring about Scrooge's reform?

Activity 9

Plan your response by firstly answering the following questions.

a) Is the emphasis here on the ghosts or on Scrooge? How do you know?

----

b) What, other than past, present and future, do the ghosts represent? How do you know?

----

c) How do these other qualities affect the methods each ghost uses in reforming Scrooge?

The answers above will give you a general structure for your answer. In your plan you can summarize this structure as bullets or put it into boxes/bubbles in a spider diagram. Then, as you write, you will need to make sure you include:

- references from the text to support your ideas
- some short quotations if possible
- the use of literary terminology to describe Dickens' technique
- some mention of context (for example, the Victorian ghost story).

Activity 10

Based on your answers to the three parts of Activity 9, produce a plan for the example exam question on page 94, using your preferred method.

NB: Do not cross out your plan – if you run out of time, the examiner may give you credit for what you would have written.

Upgrade

Examiners want to see that you have thought about the novella and can introduce your own ideas when responding to the question. So while practising exam answers is important, it is a bad idea to go in with a prepared essay, which may not be relevant to the question on the paper.

Writing your answer

Whichever exam board you are entered for, you may have a question based on an extract from *A Christmas Carol*. This will test your ability to focus closely on the text, and on the novella as a whole. It will also test your knowledge of the text and your ability to think about how Dickens has created his novella and the context in which it was written.

If the question gives bullet points to guide your answer, make sure you use these.

Consider a question like this:

Charles Dickens: *A Christmas Carol*

Read the following extract from Stave 1 and answer the questions that follow.

In this extract Scrooge has just refused his nephew's invitation to Christmas dinner.

"Don't be cross, uncle!" said the nephew.

"What else can I be," returned the uncle, "when I live in such a world of fools as this? Merry Christmas! Out upon merry Christmas! What's Christmas time to you but a time for paying bills without money; a time for finding yourself a year older, but not an hour richer; a time for balancing your books and having every item in 'em through a round dozen of months presented dead against you? If I could work my will," said Scrooge indignantly, "every idiot who goes about with 'Merry Christmas' on his lips, should be boiled with his own pudding, and buried with a stake of holly through his heart. He should!"

"Uncle!" pleaded the nephew.

"Nephew!" returned the uncle, sternly, "keep Christmas in your own way, and let me keep it in mine."

"Keep it!" repeated Scrooge's nephew. "But you don't keep it."

"Let me leave it alone, then," said Scrooge. "Much good may it do you! Much good it has ever done you!"

"There are many things from which I might have derived good, by which I have not profitted, I dare say," returned the nephew. "Christmas among the rest. But I am sure I have always thought of Christmas time, when it has come round—apart from the veneration due to its sacred name and origin, if anything belonging to it can be apart from that—as a good time; a kind, forgiving, charitable, pleasant time; the only time I know of, in the long calendar of the year, when men and women seem by one consent to open their shut-up hearts freely, and to think of people below them as if they really were fellow-passengers to the grave, and not another race of creatures bound on other journeys. And therefore, uncle, though it has never put a scrap of gold or silver in my pocket, I believe that it *has* done me good, and *will* do me good; and I say, God bless it!"

Starting with this extract, explore how Christmas is presented in *A Christmas Carol*.

Write about:

- how Dickens presents Christmas in this extract
- how Dickens presents Christmas in the novella as a whole.

Activity 11

Read the sample exam question on page 96 carefully. Before you begin, plan your answer in two parts, the first related to the extract and the second related to the whole novella, by answering the points below.

The extract

Step 1: Underline Scrooge's views on Christmas in the extract.

Step 2: Highlight Fred's views on Christmas in the extract.

Step 3: Comment briefly on which view you think Dickens wants his readers to agree with and why you think this.

Step 4: Write down three techniques used by Dickens to present Christmas in the extract.

Step 5: Write brief notes on anything that strikes you about Dickens's use of vocabulary and sentence structure in this extract.

The whole novel

Step 6: How is Scrooge's view of Christmas presented later:
- in the encounter with the charity collectors?

- in his childhood?

How does this show him as an outsider (context)?

Step 7: How is Fred's view of Christmas developed later:
- in the scene with Belle's family?

- in the Cratchits' Christmas dinner?

- in the scene with Fred's party?

Step 8: What does this suggest about the typical Victorian Christmas (context)?

Now you have an outline structure for your answer, you can begin to write it.

Think about your opening – the examiner wants to see that you have a businesslike approach. **Never** start by saying something like, 'In this answer I will…'. Instead, go straight into the subject of Christmas in the novella and how Dickens presents it.

Activity 12

Write the opening part of your answer to the question on page 96.
Remember to show that you have understood the question and noted that the extract contains different viewpoints. Use brief, embedded quotations to support your ideas. Analyse the techniques that Dickens uses to present these viewpoints (structure, form, language, humour, imagery, satire, irony, etc.). Comments on context would be helpful.

Activity 13

Look at the openings to the question on page 96 written by two different students below. Highlight and comment on how well they have/have not used all the points emphasized in Activity 12.

Student A

In my essay I will explore how Christmas is presented in the novel. In the extract it shows that Scrooge is cross and doesn't like Christmas. 'Out upon merry Christmas.' He says people who keep it are fools and should be boiled with holly stuck in them. This is Dickens using humour. His nephew takes a different view as he thinks Christmas is a great time when people think about others and have a better view of the world. These are opposite opinions and I think Dickens wants to show how mean Scrooge is and how he hates other people. He wants us to see Fred as someone who thinks about others. Scrooge only thinks about bills and money at Christmas while most people want to enjoy the time and not worry.

Student B

In the extract Dickens presents Scrooge and his nephew as having opposite views of Christmas and he structures it as an argument not merely between two ideas but between two contrasting personalities. He uses satire when he has Scrooge say that any idiot who wishes others a merry Christmas ought to be 'boiled with his own pudding, and buried with a stake of holly through his heart.' Although this metaphorical fate is intended humorously it gives an insight to Scrooge's contempt for other people.

Scrooge uses tripling to argue that Fred should balance his books – a device that is balanced in itself. Fred, on the other hand, is shown to be caring and to welcome Christmas as the season when people 'open their shut-up hearts freely' and consider others as fellows. Dickens uses a string of adjectives, 'a good time; a kind, forgiving, charitable, pleasant time' to show Fred's more emotional argument.

Dickens presents attitudes towards Christmas as indicators of character and empathy. Scrooge is shown to be out of step with the majority of Victorians who would have agreed with Fred about the Christian nature of Christmas remembering the birth of Jesus through church-going and giving to others.

You need to refer to the novel as a construct – that is something created by a writer for a purpose or to achieve a particular response, using literary techniques.

Activity 14

a) In the scene from Stave 2 where Belle and her family celebrate Christmas Eve:

i. What techniques does Dickens use to show the mother and children as noisy and happy?

----

ii. What techniques does Dickens use to show the relationship between father and children?

----

b) Although you will not be expected to remember long, detailed quotations from the novella, you will be expected to know short, relevant quotations to illustrate your point. Look at the paragraphs written by two students below. Who is better at:

i. considering the novel as a construct? _____

ii. using literary terminology? _____

Student A

Belle's children are very noisy. They rush about, acting like a herd of animals. They jump on their big sister and pull her about, but she and her mum just laugh. They probably know the children are excited about Christmas. When their dad comes home with presents they jump on him instead and grab for their parcels. Although they kick him and nearly strangle him, he doesn't seem to mind. This shows they are a happy family who love their children, but they are still glad when they go to bed. Dickens shows how they are a typical Victorian family with lots of kids who like playing games and getting Christmas presents.

Student B

Dickens presents Belle and her eldest daughter as looking alike, a device to make Scrooge regret that he is not the child's father. He shows the excitement of the younger children by comparing their behaviour with a herd as they play games and persuade their sister to join in. Dickens uses digression to suggest that Scrooge would have treated her more gently – a technique that helps to convince the reader of her reality. He tells us that mother and daughter enjoyed the children's rowdy games and laughed a lot, showing they have a good relationship.

When their father comes home with presents Dickens uses the metaphor of the father as a tower being scaled by children using chairs to reach the parcels. He employs ironic humour to show the children's love through the way they pummel, kick and strangle their father. He depicts a family that most people will understand, especially the alarm over the baby having possibly swallowed an object and the peace that descends once the children are in bed. He also uses them to present an ideal Victorian family Christmas, with the children's games and the presents being given out. Dickens later builds on this ideal when he depicts the Cratchits' Christmas dinner.

Activity 15

Write the next two paragraphs of your answer to the question you began answering in Activity 12. Consider the representations of Christmas as celebrated by the Cratchits and Fred, which Scrooge observes with the Ghost of Christmas Present. Remember to:

- relate the answer back to the question and the extract
- use textual reference and, where possible, quotation to support your points
- write about the novella as a construct including Dickens's techniques as a writer
- relate it to context as appropriate.

Upgrade

One of the main differences between middle and higher grades is the level of analysis that is used. For a good grade you need to show understanding of a writer's techniques and be able to support your views. For a high grade you need to evaluate a writer's techniques and support your answer with detailed and well-chosen references.

Finishing your answer

At the end of your answer you want to leave the examiner with a good impression. Summing up what you have already written is a waste of time – the examiner cannot award marks for repetition of points already made.

Activity 16

a) Looking back at the exam question and how you have developed your answer, write down three 'lessons' you think Dickens wanted his readers to take away from his presentation of Christmas in the novella.

----

b) Write down three pieces of evidence for your opinions.

----

c) Write down three lessons that Scrooge learned from the way Christmas is presented in the novella.

----

d) Write down three pieces of evidence for your views.

----

e) Is there an overlap between Scrooge's learning and the reader's? If so what?

----

f) In your opinion, did Dickens intend his readers to be educated about the true meaning of Christmas alongside Scrooge? Give reasons for your views.

Activity 17

Now write the final paragraph of your answer using the information learnt on pages 102-103. Remember to include writing techniques and context.

Activity 18

Try the following, on separate paper.

a) Choose two of the questions in the 'Understanding the question' part of this chapter, and produce plans for them.

b) Write two or three of your own questions, choosing appropriate extracts.

c) Practise writing a whole answer to at least one of the questions in the 'Understanding the question' part of this chapter.

Upgrade

Bear in mind that for the higher grades you will need a detailed knowledge of the text and how it is constructed. You should also demonstrate your understanding of Dickens's narrative at different levels – the story level, the social level and the spiritual and moral level. In addition, you must show you can use literary terminology fluently and use detailed and well-chosen evidence to support your ideas.

Progress check

Use the chart below to review the skills you have developed in this chapter. For each column, start at the bottom box and work your way up towards the highest level in the top box. Tick the box to show you have achieved that level.

Personal response	Textual references	Language, structure, form	Technical accuracy
I can sustain a critical response to *A Christmas Carol* and interpret the plot, characters and themes convincingly ☐	I can use well-integrated textual references from *A Christmas Carol* to support my interpretation ☐	I can analyse the effects of Dickens' use of language, structure and form in *A Christmas Carol*, using subject terms judiciously ☐	I use a wide range of vocabulary and can spell and punctuate consistently accurately ☐
I can develop a coherent response to *A Christmas Carol* and explain the plot, characters and themes clearly ☐	I can use quotations and other textual references from *A Christmas Carol* to support my explanation ☐	I can explain how Dickens uses language, structure and form to create effects in *A Christmas Carol*, using relevant subject terms ☐	I use a range of vocabulary and can spell and punctuate, mostly accurately ☐
I can make some comments on the plot, characters and themes in *A Christmas Carol* ☐	I can make references to some details from *A Christmas Carol* ☐	I can identify some of Dickens' methods in *A Christmas Carol* and use some subject terms ☐	I use a simple range of vocabulary and spell and punctuate with some accuracy ☐

Glossary

administrator   the person who actually carries out the terms of a will

allegory   a metaphorical story

alliteration   the repetition of first letters in words that follow each other

assign   the person to whom the property and affairs of the dead person are transferred

benefactor   someone who gives to or benefits others

'Change   the Royal Exchange, London's Financial centre

climax   the high point or peak of the action, after which everything changes

connotation   an image, feeling or idea associated with a word or phrase

convention   an aspect or theme that is common to the genre

denouement   the way the main character finally ends up (happily in comedy; badly in tragedy)

executor   a person responsible for seeing the terms of a will are carried out

exposition   where the author introduces the main character and the basic conflict, finishing with the event that decides the rest of the story

falling action or resolution   the final part of the conflict that decides whether the main character wins or loses

genre   the type of story, such as romance, adventure, horror, ghost story, etc.

hyperbole   exaggeration for effect

imagery   using words that create mental images

inversion   using a phrase that can have more than one meaning

metaphor   the comparison of a thing, idea or action with another (usually imagined) that is similar

onomatopoeia   a word that sounds like the thing or action it represents

parable   a story that shows a moral or spiritual lesson

personification   a comparison that gives human qualities to inanimate or abstract things

pun   a word or phrase that can have more than one meaning

qualifying word   a word that describes, such as an adjective or adverb

repetition   the repeating of words or phrases for effect

residuary legatee   the person who inherits all the estate after bills have been paid

rising action   the series of events that lead in stages up to the story's climax

simile   a comparison between two things that states one is 'like' or 'as' the other

skinflint   mean or tight-fisted person

supernatural   something that is beyond nature – seeing the spirit of a dead person, for example

OXFORD
UNIVERSITY PRESS

Great Clarendon Street, Oxford, OX2 6DP, United Kingdom

Oxford University Press is a department of the University of Oxford.
It furthers the University's objective of excellence in research, scholarship,
and education by publishing worldwide. Oxford is a registered trade mark
of Oxford University Press in the UK and in certain other countries

British Library Cataloguing in Publication Data

Data available

ISBN 978-019-839889-9

10 9 8 7 6 5 4 3 2 1

Printed in Great Britain by CPI Group (UK) Ltd., Croydon CR0 4YY

Acknowledgements

We are grateful for permission to reprint the following copyright material:

Michel Faber: extracts from 'Spectral Pleasures', review of *The Christmas
Carol, The Guardian*, 24 Dec 2005, copyright © Guardian News & Media Ltd
2005, reprinted by permission of GNM.

John Mullan: extract from 'Ghosts in *A Christmas Carol*', British Library
website, 8 May 2015, reprinted by permission of the author.

The publisher and authors would like to thank the following for
permission to use photographs and other copyright material:

Cover: © Pabkov/Shutterstock; p31(tl): Mary Evans Picture Library; p31(tr):
Amoret Tanner/Alamy Stock Photo; p31(bl): Chronicle/Alamy Stock Photo;
p31(br): Linda Steward/iStockphoto.